RECREATING THE PARISH

Reproducible Resources for Pastoral Ministers

Carol M. Holden, D.Min.
Thomas P. Sweetser, SJ
Mary Beth Vogel, MPS

Sheed and Ward
Kansas City

Copyright© 1996 by Carol M. Holden, D.Min, Thomas P. Sweetser, SJ, Mary Beth Vogel, MPS

Permission is granted to the parish institution that buys this volume for reproducing as many copies as are needed for this institution, provided that such copies are not sold. The artwork may not be reproduced apart from this *Recreating the Parish* program. No part of this book may be reproduced by other than the purchasing institution without permission in writing from the Publisher.

Sheed & Ward™ is a service of The National Catholic Reporter Publishing Company.

ISBN: 1-55612-808-8

Published by: Sheed & Ward
 115 E. Armour Blvd.
 P.O. Box 419492
 Kansas City, MO 64141-6492

To order, call: (800) 333-7373

Cover art and design by James F. Brisson.

Contents

FOREWORD v

LIST OF WORK SHEETS,
HANDOUTS AND CASE STUDIES vii

1 | LEADERSHIP AND
    MANAGEMENT 1

2 | COLLABORATION 31

3 | DECISION-MAKING 49

4 | CONFLICT
    MANAGEMENT 59

5 | STRESS
    MANAGEMENT 77

6 | PLANNING: MISSION
    AND PRESENT SITUATION 91

7 | PLANNING: VISION
    AND IMPLEMENTATION 117

8 | PLANNING: EVALUATION –
    LINKING PAST, PRESENT AND FUTURE 135

FOREWORD

One day, while Alice was walking through Wonderland, she came to a fork in the road. Puzzled, she inquired of the Cheshire Cat which road she should take. The smiling cat asked her where she was going. After a moment Alice responded, "I don't know where I am going." "Well," the cat said, "then it doesn't matter *what* path you take does it."

Like Alice, most of us get so caught up in the details of our daily lives that we forget where we are going! On the one hand, we know and believe in the value of long-range planning, empowerment of the laity and shared decision-making. On the other hand, we live in the reality of deadlines, unexpected demands and limitations of time and energy.

If there is one premise that should underlie all our work, it is that each of us is trying our best to do what we think is right. No one is *intentionally* trying to fail or cause others frustration. Sometimes we know things are just not working, or at least not working to full potential, but we don't know what to do. It is the combination of sincere desire and a need for *tools* to fulfill this desire that has led to the creation of this book.

ORIGINS

We were excited when the folks from Sheed & Ward contacted us about doing a book of reproducible exercises. People from the parishes where we have worked and those who have read our books, have often asked permission to use various processes and exercises. This book gives us an opportunity to make these resources available to a wide range of people.

Those of you who have used our material before will notice that some things have changed. We learn something new from every parish and group with whom we work. Keeping examples current and language "politically correct" can be quite a challenge. Like most publications, the minute this book goes to press it will be dated. But we do not consider this a problem, because this is not intended to be the final word on anything. These are *tools*. They will not all work in every situation nor is every group ready to carry out all the suggestions. These ideas need adjustment to fit each particular group.

What we hope you *will* find are underlying principles, basic ways of being parish, community, leaders, and people. The parishes and groups who have used these processes and work sheets have, for the most part, found them useful and exciting. New insights and better understanding gained from these exercises have led to greater communication, deeper commitment and renewed energy to move forward.

USER FRIENDLY

This book does not need to be read cover-to-cover. The table of contents gives a broad idea of the focus of each chapter. The list of Work Sheets, Handouts and Case Studies will give direction if you know what you are looking for but do not know where to find it. Many of the exercises will be found under several topic headings.

Each chapter is designed to provide background material on the topic and practical exercises that bring these theories to life. An introductory story or example opens each chapter to set the stage. The topic is expanded to include brief explanations and use of the reproducible sheets. Three types of sheets are included here: work sheets, handouts, case studies.

Work Sheets are pages that involve some type of written work. Directions appear at the top of each sheet for use independently of the explanation pages. As with all the materials, feel free to adjust the directions depending on your situation. The communication of ideas and feelings is the primary purpose of this work.

Handouts are pages that, in their present format, do not require any written work. These can be used as discussion starters, reminder sheets, or explanations of broad topics. Feel free to create exercises that might bring this material to life for your group.

Case Studies are simply stories, yet they reveal much about your group as you struggle with the role-play, dialogue or situation. The scenarios will sound familiar because these, too, are reflections of real experiences we have had or heard about. The value of case studies is that these stories allow groups to talk about events and learn skills before struggling with their own issues. They provide a safe environment in which to learn.

Each chapter concludes with a list of references. These resources will provide you with more background information and practical suggestions in each area.

READY, SET, GO

We cannot emphasize enough how important it is that you make all these exercises and experiences your own. When we visit parishes there are always those people who want us to *fix* their pastor, council, staff, or community. We are not there to *fix* anything or anyone. What we do provide are the *tools*. It is up to you to use what is helpful to your community and see where you can go. The blessing is in the effort. Others have struggled before you and more will continue in the future. Now venture ahead and good luck!

ACKNOWLEDGEMENTS

It seems to have become quite fashionable to give *glory to God* for every game won, award presented or accomplishment achieved. Not a bad trend! Anyone who has worked on a *team* knows that the reality is much more difficult than the rhetoric. Writing a book is no exception. That is why we too must thank, first and foremost, a very good and gracious God for bringing us to this point *together*.

There are also many who had a hand in developing the processes and exercises. As we said earlier, everywhere we go we are challenged and intrigued by what people are doing every day in parishes. To these folks and their creative efforts we say thank you.

Ideas are one thing, turning them into a finished product is another. Special thanks to all who helped in the development of this book. We are indebted to Management Design Institute of Cincinnati, Ohio, for some of the foundational concepts and approaches for Work Sheets **6-F** and **6-G** from Chapter 6. We would also like to thank those who "shared their wisdom" in bringing the book into final form: Mary Borowicz, Kristin and Mark Garstki, Kathleen Hage, Tom Holden, Dolores Stanton, Mary Ziegler and Jeanne and Marius Zurat. May God bless you for all your encouragement and support.

LIST OF WORK SHEETS, HANDOUTS AND CASE STUDIES

Chapter One: Leadership and Management
    Leading And Managing   1-A
    A Reflection On Leadership   1-B
    Continuum Of Leadership Behavior   1-C
    The Facilitating Leader   1-D1 & 1-D2
    Leadership Role-Play   1-E1 - 1-E11
    Leadership Flow   1-F
    Managing Structures   1-G
    Work Sheet For Managing Structures   1-H
    Managing Staff And Council Meetings   1-I
    Agenda For Parish Staff Meeting   1-J1 & 1-J2
    Five Factors Of Motivation   1-K
    Motivations For Ministry   1-L
    The Positive Use Of Power   1-M
    Managing The Image   1-N
    An Exercise In Image Building   1-O

Chapter Two: Collaboration
    Collaboration   2-A
    Mutuality   2-B
    Identifying Gifts   2-C
    Stages Of Community Growth   2-D
    Partnership   2-E
    Reflection On Partnership   2-F
    Sharing Wisdom   2-G
    "Sane" Approach To Partnership   2-H
    Helps For Improving Collaborative Ministry   2-I
    Group Dynamics   2-J
    A Partnership Fantasy   2-K
    Collaboration: Some Win...   2-L1 & 2-L2
    Case Study On Collaboration   2-M1 & 2-M2

Chapter Three: Decision Making
    Step-By-Step With C - D - I   3-A
    Levels Of Decision Making   3-B
    Problem Solving Process   3-C
    Discernment Work Sheet   3-D
    Discernment Process For Council Chairperson   3-E
    Exploring Past Decisions   3-F

Chapter Four: Conflict Management
    How Do You Usually Handle Conflicts?   4-A
    Looking At The Conflict   4-B
    Work Sheet On Conflict Management   4-C
    Appropriate Style Of Conflict Management   4-D
    Practicing Conflict: Case Study One   4-E1 & 4-E2
    Practicing Conflict: Case Study Two   4-F1 & 4-F2
    Practicing Conflict: Case Study Three   4-G1 & 4-G2
    Observer Work Sheet (A)   4-H
    Group Case Study: Situation One   4-I
    Group Case Study: Situation Two   4-J
    Group Case Study: Situation Three   4-K
    Group Case Study: Situation Four   4-L
    Observer Work Sheet (B)   4-M

Chapter Five: Stress Management
    How Stress-Resistant Are You?   5-A
    Stress Exhaustion Symptoms   5-B
    AAAbc's Of Stress Management   5-C
    AAAbc's Of Stress Management Work Sheet   5-D
    AAAbc Application Forms   5-E - 5-I
    Burnout Prevention: Taking Your Pulse . . .   5-J

Chapter Six: Planning: Mission and Present Situation
    Spirituality   6-A
    Assessing Our Level of Spirituality   6-B
    Whatsit   6-C1 - 6-C4
    Elements Of A Mission Statement   6-D
    Process For Arriving At A Mission Statement   6-E1 & 6-E2
    Where Have We Come From? Where Are We Now?   6-F
    Reflection Questions On Present Situation   6-G
    Information Gathering   6-H1 & 6-H2
    Census Update   6-I1 & 6-I2
    Suggestions For Surveying   6-J1 & 6-J2
    Establishing A Hierarchy Of Needs   6-K
    Suggestions For Parish Town Hall Meetings   6-L1 & 6-L2

Chapter Seven: Planning: Vision and Implementation
    Response Process   7-A1 & 7-A2
    Guidelines For Parish Action Plans   7-B
    Work Sheet For Scenario Building   7-C
    Translating Dreams Into Action   7-D1 - 7-D3
    Gonna-Be   7-E1 & 7-E2
    Volunteer Case Studies   7-F
    Job Description Sheet   7-G
    Personal Preferences Of Volunteers   7-H
    Rewards And Benefits For Volunteers   7-I

Chapter Eight: Planning: Evaluation – Linking Past, Present and Future
    Reviewing The Evaluation Process   8-A
    Job Description   8-B1 & 8-B2
    Feedback On The . . .   8-C1 - 8-C3
    Ministry Evaluation   8-D
    Evaluation Form   8-E
    Evaluation Of A Volunteer Ministry   8-F1 & 8-F2
    Evaluation Of . . .   8-G

1 | LEADERSHIP AND MANAGEMENT

INTRODUCTION Leadership pushes the boundaries, expands the horizons, seeks a vision of what could be. It challenges a group to grow, to leave the familiar and try out new ways of doing things. Leadership includes not only the designated leader but the group as well. The two influence each other as they seek a new reality and a change in the present situation.

Jesus was a leader who called people to a new way of living. But he was also influenced by the people around him as they helped shape his mission and call. They longed for freedom, for less oppression, for a better life. Jesus offered a way out of the bondage and routine. Jesus was the bearer of their dream and the instigator of change.

Management is a different dynamic. It includes all the organizing and coordinating necessary to bring a task to completion. "Managers" see to it that the task is accomplished. They also enlist others, whenever necessary, to make sure it gets done well and within required limits.

A good example of management in the New Testament is the appointment of deacons in the sixth chapter of Acts. A problem of caring for the Greek widows arose and the deacons were organized to handle this need. Leadership points the way. Management helps the group get there.

Suppose the pastor returns from a four-month sabbatical in which he experienced a new and vital way of being church. He calls together the staff and council and shares with them his vision for a parish that is alive and exciting. Others get caught up in the pastor's enthusiasm. It prompts them all to dream about what could happen in the parish. Together they paint the picture of what the parish *could be* in the next three to five years. The liturgies are upbeat, the adult formation exciting, the outreach into the community significant and effective. The inactive and unchurched are encouraged to return to this new way of being church.

The staff and council share this vision of the parish with other groups and leaders. The pastor proclaims it from the pulpit and writes about it in the bulletin. This is the essence of leadership, creating and sharing a vision of what *could be* and calling for a change from the status quo.

Once the group knows where it wants to go, management provides the means for putting the plan into action. It includes all the organizing, motivating, directing and supporting needed to realize the dream. Once the pastor, staff and council know what path to follow, they identify the tasks that need to be accomplished. These are then delegated to the various committees, ministries and organizations in the parish.

Work Sheet **1-A** provides an exercise that helps clarify the amount of time one spends in leading and in managing. It assists people in identifying their use of time relative to their gifts and desires.

WHO IS INVOLVED IN LEADERSHIP?

Creating a vision and challenging a group to change belongs to more than the leader. Three other elements are important: the interaction of the leader and the group, the environment in which the group operates and the spirit of the group. When speaking of spirit, this includes both the camaraderie of the group and the inspiration of the Holy Spirit. The Spirit can sometimes take the leadership beyond what it thought possible and suggest new heights to explore. Work Sheet **1-B** provides a method for identifying these aspects of leadership.

There is not one way of leading. The pastor who returned from a sabbatical could have gathered the staff and council together and *announced* to the group that he had a new vision of parish and from now on this is what would be expected of them as parish leaders. He could also have tried to *convince* them of the merits of his new approach, having made the decision beforehand but wanting them to think it was their idea as well. He could have *presented* his new plan to the leaders and invited their questions and reactions. This discussion may have altered his vision but it remained *his* vision, not the staff's and council's. Another choice would have been to keep the vision to himself and try to operate in a new way, hoping that the leaders and people would catch the fire through his example and by osmosis rather than by direct involvement in the new direction.

Instead, the pastor chose another approach, one that he learned on his sabbatical. In calling the staff and council together he *shared* his vision with them and asked for their visions of the parish as well. Using his new insights as a spark, he divided the people into groups of threes and fours. He invited them to construct a scenario of what could happen in the parish. His style of leading was as a facilitator or *sparker*, rather than as the sole "owner" of the vision. The leaders responded well to this approach. As one person remarked, "It was like taking the lid off of the pan and letting all the creative juices flow." Work Sheet **1-C** provides an exercise for helping individuals and groups identify their predominant style of leading and the style with which people may feel most comfortable.

WHO IS INVOLVED IN LEADERSHIP?

Although all types of leading are appropriate at one time or another. One type has proven to be the most successful for encouraging involvement and ownership by the participants. It is a *facilitating* style of leading. This is the method the pastor used in the example given above. Work Sheets **1-D1** and **1-D2** provide the Do's and Don'ts for this way of leading, based on the Planning Cycle described in Chapter Six. The facilitating leader still exercises strong leadership but not of the authoritarian or manipulative variety. Learning how to involve the group without coercion or taking over requires practice. Section **1-E** is a roleplay exercise that provides an opportunity for experiencing different styles of leadership. It is meant to prompt discussion and feedback about present styles of leadership operative in the parish or organization.

Different gifts and preferences play into the leadership mix. Some people are better dreamers or visionaries. Others do better at goal-setting and focusing the dream. Still, others prefer the hands-on, concrete side of leadership. Harmonizers constitute a fourth group. They are able to provide leadership by getting everyone to work well together, and reducing the friction between groups.

Suppose one aspect of the new vision for parish is a change in the worship space. The setting for Mass is flexible with moveable chairs but something is missing. The liturgy commission is given the job of making it better. A few people in the group are good *DREAMERS*. They inspire others by brainstorming, surfacing new ideas and options. As these ideas start flowing, a few others start narrowing the options and move the group toward a focused plan. These are the *GOAL-SETTERS*. As a new arrangement of altar and chairs begins to emerge, others in the group offer suggestions as to how to move the plan closer to reality. They are the *ACTION-TAKERS*. A few others keep supporting the movement of the group, providing words of support, encouragement and enthusiasm. These are the *HARMONIZERS*. Each person plays a part as the plan moves from dream to reality. Work Sheet **1-F** provides an exercise for uncovering one's primary and secondary preference for leading.

Note: All four aspects of leading are necessary for the productive functioning of a group. To ask one person, such as the pastor or chairperson, to perform all four functions of *dreamer, goal-setter, action-taker* and *harmonizer* is unrealistic and leads to burnout. Better to uncover people's gifts and empower group members to assume different leadership functions at each stage of the plan's development. The more participating in the leadership interaction, the more successful and enjoyable the outcome.

HOW DOES MANAGEMENT HAPPEN?

Leadership points the way. Where does the group want to go, what does it want to shoot for, what changes are necessary to move from the present position to the desired outcome? Management includes all the skills, techniques and strategies for reaching the dream.

Management is not a simple concept. It includes a number of aspects. To be successful in managing a group, a number of issues need to be addressed. These include managing *structures, human resources, politics* and *symbols* or *image*.

MANAGING STRUCTURES

The first task is to manage the *structures*. Suppose part of the new vision adopted by the pastor, staff and council is to deepen the sense of community and belonging among the parishioners. People want to come to the parish and feel "at home," accepted and comfortable. The task is to create this climate of friendliness and welcoming. In drawing the present structure of the parish as suggested by Work Sheet **1-G**, the leaders discover that there is no group in the parish responsible for fostering community. Creating a sense of warmth and friendliness is part of the mission of many parish ministries and organizations, but there is no one group that is responsible for "managing" this important area of parish life.

A work group was created by the council and given the task of forming structures that would foster a better community spirit in the parish. Using the Work Sheet for Managing Structures (**1-H**), the task group called together all the groups and organizations associated with building community, such as the women's club, the singles' group, the greeters, the seniors, the small faith communities and the social committee. They listened to each group explain how it contributes to the spirit of friendliness and welcoming in the parish. From this group, they asked for volunteers to form a Community Life Coordinating Group that would meet monthly to foster a new spirit of community and fun in the parish.

One of the first duties of this coordinating group was to reorganize the parish calendar so that there was more sharing instead of a competition among organizations for meeting rooms and fund-raisers. This new Community Life group was linked into the council through a representative and given a staff contact person as a resource.

This is one example of managing structures well. All aspects of parish life that include forming missions statements, setting goals, organizing groups, clarifying roles, forming committees and linking groups together are part of managing parish structures well. Even organizing meetings is part of this area. One way of doing this is suggested by Work Sheets **1-I**, **1-J1** and **1-J2**.

MANAGING HUMAN RESOURCES

Human resources is a second aspect of management. It involves all the ways of motivating and inspiring people in their ministry. It helps people feel a strong sense of ownership. It addresses such questions as: Are ministers given recognition and affirmation in their work? Do they have a chance to socialize and share experiences with others? Do they feel a sense of growth and personal development?

Creating a conducive and supportive environment helps people feel motivated and productive in their ministry. Examples of a parish that manages its human resources well might include the weekly choir practice that becomes a social event as well as a chance to learn new music. The monthly gathering of pastoral care ministers becomes a small faith community as they reflect on their care for the sick. The planning meeting for the annual parish mission becomes a religious experience as the planners reflect on relevant themes. These are a few examples of well-managed interactions among pastoral ministers. Work Sheets **1-K** and **1-L** provide reflection exercises that can serve as checklists for those involved in the management of human resources. Work sheets contained in other chapters of this book also serve as additional resources.

MANAGING POLITICS

This is an aspect of management that is often overlooked in pastoral settings. "Love one another" is the ideal, but the reality does not always measure up to this Gospel imperative. The imposition of authority, the limitation of funding or the shortage of space can lead to conflicts and power struggles. It is at these moments that the management of politics becomes essential.

One aspect of managing politics is dealing with conflicts that arise among those involved in ministry. This is such an important area that an entire chapter is devoted to this subject. [See Chapter Four.]

Another aspect of managing politics is the positive use of power in ministerial situations. Too often power is seen in a negative light with coercive or limiting qualities. "The pastor has all the power and I don't have the freedom to do my work." "The religious education director is always looking over my shoulder and I am not free to make my own decisions in the classroom." "The ushers don't ever let us stand in the back entrance and watch Mass through the glass doors."

But power also has a positive connotation. This use of power taps into the talents and abilities of the group and opens up opportunities to accomplish tasks not otherwise possible. Work Sheet **1-M** describes a process for tapping into the positive aspects of power.

MANAGING THE IMAGE

The attention a parish or area of ministry gives to managing its image has much to do with how successful it will be. If people feel good about the parish, they tend to support and take part in its programs, projects and services. Image can be managed through signs, symbols, rituals and storytelling.

Notice how businesses sell their products through music, logos, slogans and graphics. Much of Jesus' proclamation of the Good News was done with images through parables and stories. The same emphasis should be given to image building in the parish. If it isn't planned and managed by those in charge, it will be created for them by the perceptions of those involved or by outside forces.

Consider the case of a parish finance board that is sensitive to the needs of the parish and the surrounding community. It guarantees that a percentage of the income is given to worthy causes and that parish ministries are well-funded. Nevertheless, it is perceived by many of the parishioners as a power group that keeps control of the purse strings. Another example might be the Women's Guild that helps support the school and parish through fund-raisers. It is perceived by many outsiders as a closed group of elderly women who only like to work on crafts and socialize together. The Rite of Reconciliation can be a wonderful sacrament of healing and grace. It is often perceived as a threatening exercise of guilt and penance.

Work Sheet **1-N** provides a means for uncovering various perceptions of image, both from within and from outside the group. Work Sheet **1-O** suggests a group activity that emphasizes positive image building that could lead to the management of image and symbol in a parish setting.

CONCLUSION

Leadership helps determine what direction the parish should be taking. Management helps it reach its goals and objectives. *Both* are necessary if a parish is to be successful in the modern world. All leadership and no management means the parish has great dreams but no way of realizing them. All management and no leadership means the parish is functioning smoothly but is on a plateau with no urgency or impetus for change. The work sheets that follow are offered as aids to help a parish deal with both of these important ingredients of parish life.

ADDITIONAL RESOURCES

Drucker, Peter F., *Managing the Nonprofit Organization*. NY: Harper Collins Publishers. 1990.

Lee, Harris W., *Effective Church Leadership, A Practical Sourcebook*. Minneapolis: Augsburg Press. 1989.

Parsons, George and Speed B. Leas, *Understanding Your Congregation as a System*. Washington, DC: Alban Institute. 1993.

Rost, Joseph C., *Leadership For The Twenty-First Century*. NY: Praeger Press. 1991.

Sweetser, SJ, Thomas P. and Carol M. Holden, *Leadership In A Successful Parish*, Sheed & Ward, Kansas City, 1987, 1992. Chapters Two, Four and Preface.

Sweetser, SJ, Thomas P. and Patricia M. Forster, OSF, *Transforming the Parish, Models For The Future*. Kansas City: Sheed & Ward. 1993. Chapters Four and Six.

Teston, Kevin, *Creative Christian Leadership: Skills For More Effective Ministry*. Mystic, CT: 23rd Publications. 1995.

Whitehead, James D. and Evelyn Eaton Whitehead, *The Emerging Laity*. Garden City, NY: Doubleday & Company, Inc. 1986.

LEADING AND MANAGING

Leadership deals with vision and change. It calls people to move from what is to what could be, to move from the present situation into a new future, to move toward the fulfillment of their goals and desires. **Management** deals with implementation. It gets the tasks accomplished, provides the services, maintains the operation.

Reflect on your own ministry.

1. How much of your time is spent in pastoral *leadership* and how much in pastoral *management*? Draw a line to indicate the ratio of time spent in *leading* and *managing*. Moving the line down means more time is spent managing. Moving the line up means more time is spent leading.

2. Are you satisfied with this ratio? How does it utilize your gifts and match your desires? Draw another line between managing and leading where you would *like* it to be.

3. Who are good leaders and who are good managers in your group or ministry? How are their gifts being utilized?

Share the results of this reflection with others.

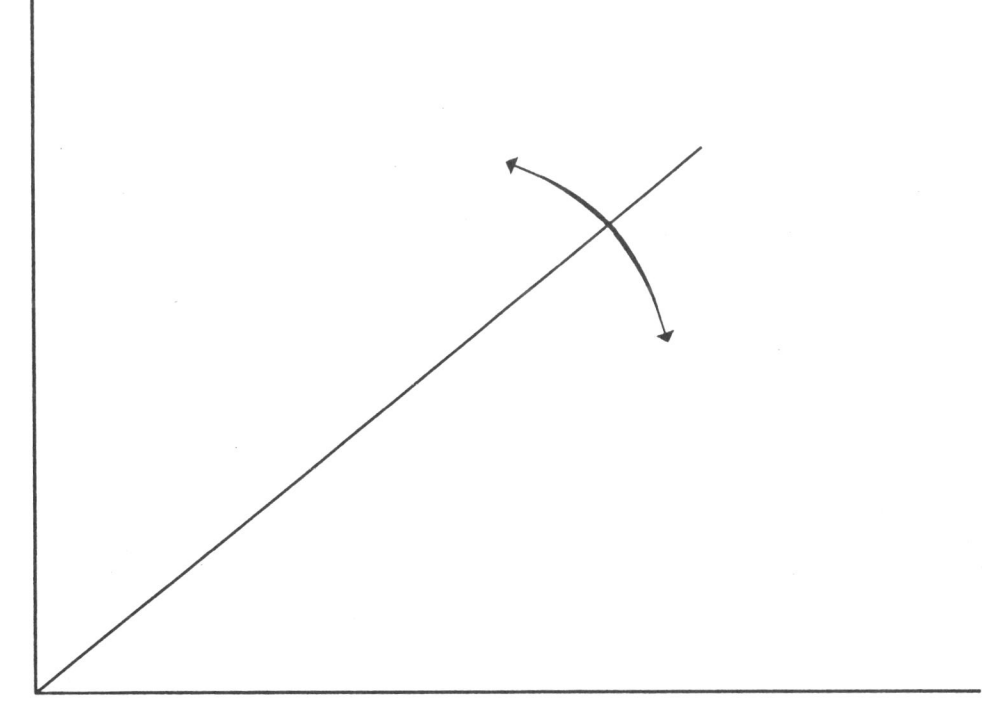

LEADING

MANAGING

A REFLECTION ON LEADERSHIP

Leadership is more than just the leader. It involves the interaction of the *LEADER, PEOPLE, ENVIRONMENT,* and *SPIRIT*. Think of one recent experience in which you were involved in leading a group. It can be either a positive (everything turned up roses) or a negative (am I glad that's over) experience.

1. Fill in your description of what was happening in each of the four areas.
2. How did each contribute toward making the situation a positive or negative experience?
3. What changes could be made to improve the leadership interaction?
4. Compare your insights with others involved in leadership situations.

(S)sPIRIT
Describe the spirit or energy of the group at the time, as well as the influence of the Holy Spirit

_____
_____

LEADER
Describe your own traits, your talents, limitations, expectations in leading the group

_____
_____

PEOPLE
Describe the type of people involved, their background, desires, age, education etc.

_____
_____

ENVIRONMENT
Describe the atmosphere where you led a group, size of room, arrangement, warmth, etc.

_____
_____

CONTINUUM OF LEADERSHIP BEHAVIOR

Leadership involves the interaction of the leader and the group as revealed by how decisions are made. There are varying degrees of authority exercised by the leader and freedom available to the group members when making decisions. Think of your own group and place an X on the diagonal line that describes the present interaction of the leader and the group members. Place an O where you would like the interaction to be. Share this with one other person in the group and see if the two of you agree. Discuss the results in the group as a whole. If the group wants to move from its present place to another, what changes or commitments might be necessary?

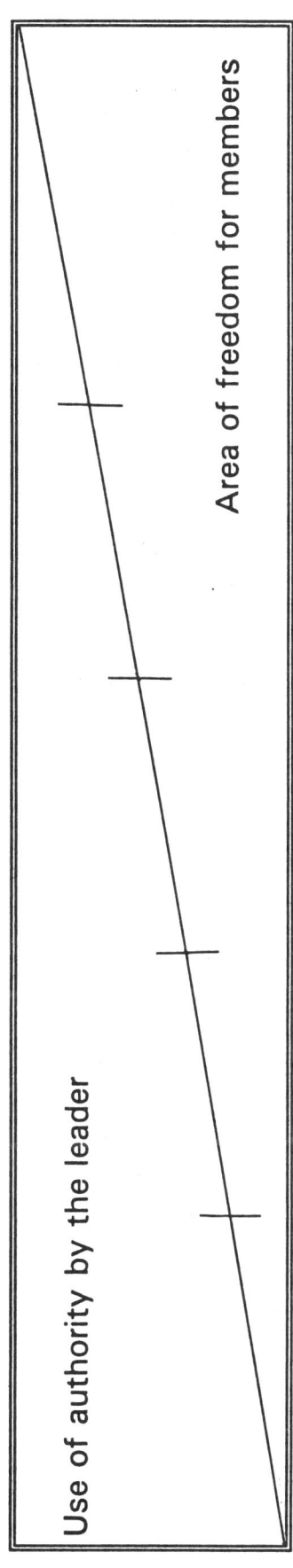

STYLE:

TELLING	SELLING	TESTING	CONSULTING	FACILITATING	JOINING
Leader makes decision and announces it to the group	Leader makes decision and "sells" it to the group	Leader presents tentative decision, invites questions from the group, then decides	Leader presents problem to the group, gets suggestions, then makes decision	Leader sets the tone and provides the environment. Leader and group together come to a decision	Leader gives up the leadership role. The group makes the decision with no designated leader

Adapted from *Let My People Go, Empowering Laity For Ministry*, Alvin J. Lindgren & Norman Shawchuck, Nashville: Abingdon Press, 1980, p. 41.

THE FACILITATING LEADER

Use this sheet to reflect on how well you are fulfilling your role as a facilitating leader.

To those who want to be facilitating leaders:

DO:

1. Set up the environment ahead of time so that people feel they are equals with you and not that you are the controlling person. For a small group, this means sitting in a circle or around a table, allowing room for newcomers, creating a comfortable but productive atmosphere. If it is a large group, dispense with a podium or desk which separates you from the group.

2. Take the lead in getting the session or meeting started. Let people know what is expected of them and give them the opportunity to tell you what their expectations might be. Keep people on track if they wander. Bring in people who are holding back and be gentle but firm with people who are talking too much or dominating the meeting.

3. Use strategies that utilize the talents and resources of the group, such as asking each person to write down personal reflections or ideas on index cards and allowing each person to speak in turn. Or, divide the participants into groups of twos or threes so that more people can take part in the interaction.

4. Encourage people to take ownership of the meeting, issue or problem to be solved. If the task is information gathering, stimulate people to creative thinking by means of brainstorming, help them envision the ideal to work towards, or divide them into smaller task groups.

5. Once enough information is available, lead the group through the decision-making stage, making sure that everyone's opinions are respected and supported. Stay away from voting unless it is a small matter or when there is general agreement. Instead, stay with the decision until all can accept and work on the result or solution decided upon. If no conclusion can be reached, don't let the majority force the issue in the last minutes of the meeting. Put the decision off to the next meeting or ask for more time to settle the issue before the end of the meeting.

6. Once a decision has been reached, be sure that everyone knows what the next steps will be, what each committee or individual is required to accomplish and by when. The task belongs to them but your job is to hold them accountable and to keep the lines of communication open between the subgroups and participants.

7. Monitor the progress of the group so that people feel supported, listened to, encouraged to share their talents and are given rewards for their involvement and dedication. Be sure there is adequate time for socializing before, during and after the gathering, that humor is encouraged at the appropriate times, and tasks are accomplished.

8. Above all, set the tone of the gathering, one that says "we are in this together; we will get our work done but we will have fun at it at the same time." It is not necessary that you be "in charge" but rather that you provide the framework and limits for the people's interaction.

To those who want to be facilitating leaders:

DON'T:

1. Give up your role as leader, thinking that a facilitating style means giving up your leadership. You must still provide active leadership, but not in a style that is dictatorial or controlling. Your role is to set the group free to do their work and enjoy themselves, but freedom is not without limits or direction.

2. Rush in to fill vacuums created by lack of attendance, commitment or ownership. Far better to let the project fail, and in this way demonstrate that it belongs to the people and not just to you. Encourage and support, but don't take upon your shoulders the responsibilities others have assumed.

3. Become impatient with the slow process of information gathering or decision-making. Give people time to find out for themselves what is available or what options are present, even if you think you know the answers ahead of time. Don't let people force a decision before everyone has had a chance to be part of it. The time spent in trying to reach a consensus will save much time in the implementation.

4. Don't take over when the group begins going in a direction you least expected or wanted. This is the risk of facilitating leadership; it lets the people become co-leaders with you and they might be able to do it better than you. Let it happen and let go. It is the proof that you are doing your job well.

LEADERSHIP ROLE-PLAY

Set-up: The ideal number of players for this exercise is 10. It can be played with 8 or 9 players by eliminating one or two of the role cards. It can be played with more than 10 by having the extra people act as observers for one of the four parts, and then replacing participants for the other parts of the role-play. Set up a table that is large enough to accommodate 10 chairs. Using the place cards on page 2 of this section, cut up the ten name cards and fold them so they stand up on the table. The place cards are arranged around the table in the following manner:

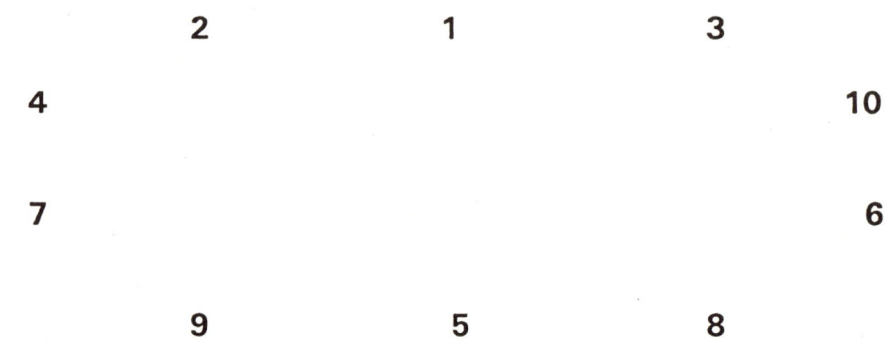

Note: The name cards stay in the same place throughout all four parts of the role-play. The players get up and change places around the table when they assume different roles.

Getting Started: Cut out the ten role cards on page 3 of this section. Let every person pick a card. They then sit around the table at the places designated for their roles. Place the *DICTATOR MODEL* sheet in the center of the table. This sheet can be enlarged for easier playing.

Process: Beginning with the pastor (1), each player reads in turn his or her role card out loud and then places it on the playing board face up over the number that matches the role-playing card. The players are only able to speak to those they are connected to by lines. In this case, everyone is able to speak to the pastor but to no one else. The observer speaks to no one but makes sure that everyone speaks only to the pastor. The observer also keeps track of the time. One person at the table reads the description of the **Dictator Model**. The observer then reads the Case Study entitled "Older Parish With Blessed Mother Statue" found on page 8 of this section. After reading the Case Study out loud to the group, the observer allows **5 MINUTES** for the participants to interact in the role play. The observer then calls **TIME** and gives reactions to the dynamics of the group and asks the participants to give their feedback as well. The purpose of this discussion is not to talk about the Case Study but to provide insight into how it felt to operate within this model of leadership.

After five to ten minutes of discussion, the role cards are collected off the playing board, shuffled and redistributed to the participants. If someone receives the same role as before, the person puts it back and chooses another role. The *PYRAMID MODEL* sheet is now placed in the center of the table and once again, each person reads the role card and places it face up on the board, pointing to the persons he or she is connected to by lines. These are the only people the person can talk with during the role-play. The description of the Pyramid Model is read out loud and the observer then reads the case study entitled "Middle Class Parish With Pro-Life Group." The group begins the role-play while the observer makes note of the time. The observer calls **TIME** after **5 Minutes** and provides feedback about the interaction and invites others to do the same. The third and fourth models follow the same procedure, making sure that people move to different places around the table as they take on different roles. The *CROWD* model uses the role-play entitled "Active Parish With Scheduling Conflict" and the *CIRCLE* model uses the one entitled "City Parish With Lay Minister Situation." In the *CIRCLE* model everyone is permitted to speak to everyone else around the table. The discussion that follows each model should include connections to the participants' current situation and to what degree each model is operative in real life.

PASTOR (1)	LITURGY DIRECTOR (6)
ASSOCIATE PASTOR (2)	YOUTH MINISTER (7)
PASTORAL ASSOCIATE (3)	PASTORAL COUNCIL PRESIDENT (8)
PRINCIPAL (4)	PERMANENT DEACON (9)
RELIGIOUS ED. COORDINATOR (5)	OBSERVER (10)

1-E2

1-E3

I AM THE PRINCIPAL OF THE SCHOOL. I AM 41 YEARS OLD.	I AM THE PRESIDENT OF THE PASTORAL COUNCIL. I AM 46 YEARS OLD.

I AM THE PASTORAL ASSOCIATE OF THE PARISH. I AM 54 YEARS OLD.	I AM THE YOUTH DIRECTOR OF THE PARISH. I AM 26 YEARS OLD.	I AM THE OBSERVER OF THE GROUP. MY AGE IS A SECRET.

I AM THE ASSOCIATE PASTOR OF THE PARISH. I AM 34 YEARS OLD.	I AM THE DIRECTOR OF LITURGY AND LITURGICAL MUSIC IN THE PARISH. I AM 39 YEARS OLD.

I AM THE PASTOR OF THE PARISH. I AM 59 YEARS OLD.	I AM THE COORDINATOR OF THE RELIGIOUS EDUCATION PROGRAM. I AM 46 YEARS OLD.	I AM THE PERMANENT DEACON OF THE PARISH. I AM 62 YEARS OLD.

Dictator Model

According to this model of decision-making the pastor is in direct contact with all levels of the parish and makes decisions based on direct information from all members of the staff and lay leaders. The focus of authority is the pastor. All others talk only to the pastor and not to each other.

Pyramid Model

According to this model of decision-making, the pastor makes the final decisions after consultation with the associates and principal, who receive ideas and suggestions from other staff members and lay leaders. There is a well-ordered distribution of authority from number 1 to number 9. The pastor talks only to the principal and associates, who in turn talk to others related to their work.

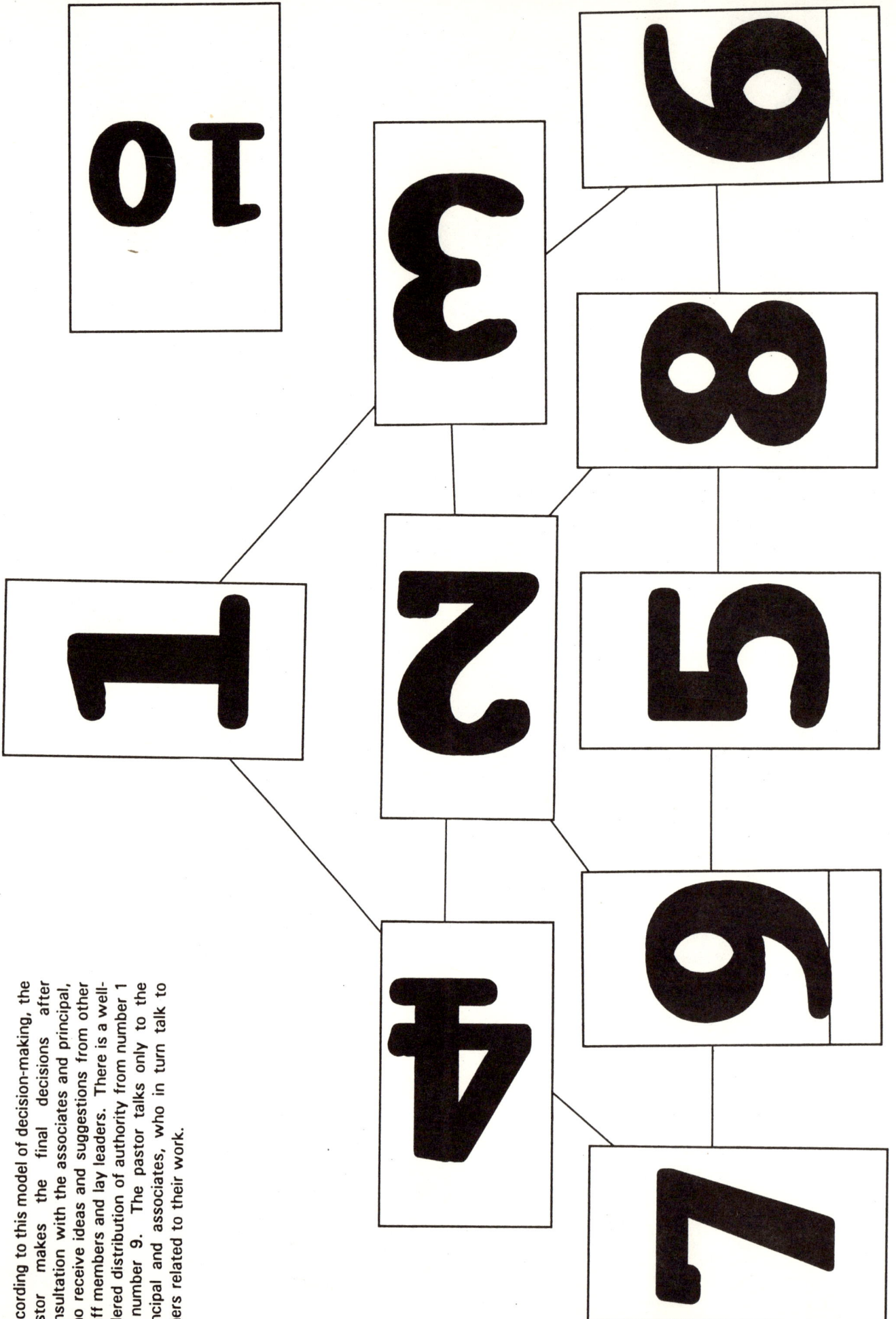

Circle Model

According to this model of decision-making, the staff and lay leaders of the parish share the authority and the running of the parish as a whole. The attempt is made to reach a consensus on parish matters so that everyone can live with the decision that is made. Everyone is free to talk to everyone else at the table.

Errata
Page 1-E7 is missing from the text.
The reverse is a replacement page provided for your use.

Crowd Model

According to this model of decision-making, everyone has an area of responsibility and the reason for coming together is to let one another know what each is doing or to resolve conflicts over scheduling and use of meeting rooms. Everyone does his or her own thing and ultimate authority resides in whoever can get the most support or wield the most influence. Staff members and lay leaders talk only to selected other people, and sometimes many conversations may be going on at once.

OLDER PARISH WITH BLESSED MOTHER STATUE

St. Anthony Parish is a mixture of all ages and backgrounds. It has just celebrated its 100th anniversary and traditions go back to the origins of the Catholic migrations of the last century.

One of the traditions is a statue of the Blessed Mother that occupies a privileged position to the left of the main altar. When the altar was moved down closer to the people, so was the statue. There is a special committee of the Altar and Rosary Society that takes care of the statue and sees to it that there are always candles burning in front of it.

Some of the staff members, however, find the statue distracting to the liturgies and were looking for a way to retire the statue. The opportunity came last month when a storm and violent winds blew out one of the windows in the church and in a flurry of song sheets and flying glass, the pedestal supporting Our Lady was shaken and the statue toppled to the ground, breaking into a number of pieces.

The Altar and Rosary Society went to work immediately repairing the statue and now want to have a special ceremony for enshrining the statue in its rightful position next to the altar. One of the staff members, however, has made it public that this is a clear sign from above that the statue is no longer supposed to adorn the sanctuary and suggested a corner in the back of the church instead. The pastor is trying to stall and figure out what to do. The Altar and Rosary Society is now threatening to cancel the annual parish social they sponsor unless the matter is settled.

A special meeting of the parish leadership has been called to figure out what to do. Reflect on this from your position in the parish and then solve it!

OBSERVER
- Be sure people talk only to those they are connected to by lines
- Pay attention to how people interact rather than the subject matter
- Notice which people talk and which are silent and why
- Notice those who are making the decisions and those who are left out

STOP the game after five minutes

- Share your observations with the group
- Invite the participants to share their reflections and feelings

1-E9

 ## *MIDDLE CLASS PARISH WITH PRO-LIFE GROUP*

Assumption Parish is a suburban parish with a large percentage of well-educated, professional parishioners. There is a high level of lay participation in the parish which pleases the staff and lay leaders. One of the more active groups is the Pro-Life group that has been encouraging parishioners to take an active stand against abortion. The group wishes the priests would preach more on the subject in their homilies. The priests feel there are other topics that also need emphasis and are somewhat concerned about the sometimes heavy-handed methods of the Pro-Life group.

Matters have come to a head during the last month when the group decided to take on the local abortion clinic. The Pro-Life group decided to picket the clinic and the event made the evening TV news. The pastor then received a call from the director of the clinic to say that the pastor would be served a civil suit for destroying the reputation of the clinic since the pastor was the official head of the parish that sponsored the picketing. The director made it clear that nothing the clinic was doing was illegal or out of line with government policy.

The Pro-Life group was delighted that they were having that much of an influence and encouraged the pastor and the staff in the fight against abortion. The parish as a whole is divided. Some of the people are backing the Pro-Life group while others complain that this has given the parish a bad name. The deadline set by the clinic for filing the suit comes up next week.

You have gathered together as the parish leadership to deal with this matter. Reflect on it from your area of ministry in the parish and then solve it!

OBSERVER
- Be sure people talk only to those they are connected to by lines
- Pay attention to how people interact rather than the subject matter
- Notice which people talk and which are silent and why
- Notice those who are making the decisions and those who are left out

STOP the game after five minutes

- Share your observations with the group
- Invite the participants to share their reflections and feelings

ACTIVE PARISH WITH SCHEDULING CONFLICT

St. James Parish is blessed with many organizations and programs. There are a number of active groups in the parish, including the Knights of Columbus, Women's Club, Charismatic Renewal, Marriage Encounter, Bible Study and Social Service. The parish buildings are in use night and day and the calendar is filled a year in advance.

The staff and council are pleased by the activity, but would like more communication between the groups. Every group seems to have its own turf. The only time the leaders of the organizations come together is at the annual calendar party. Each group spells out its activities for the coming year and parish buildings needed for their functions.

That meeting was held last month and though it started out innocently enough, it ended up a disaster. The Renewal group accused the Social Service committee of getting involved in politics. The Marriage Encounter accused the Charismatics of all show and no depth. The Women's Club president accused the Marriage Encounter group of theatrics and the Knights accused all the groups of using bad language.

This release of tension between the groups, while shocking to the participants, was helpful in uncovering a need for better communication and sharing in the parish. At the same time, the parish organizations are distrustful of each other and needless to say, the yearly calendar was not settled upon at the meeting.

The parish staff and lay leaders have decided to come together and talk about what could be done to deal with this situation. You are now at that meeting. Reflect on the problem and then solve it!

OBSERVER
- Be sure people talk only to those they are connected to by lines
- Pay attention to how people interact rather than the subject matter
- Notice which people talk and which are silent and why
- Notice those who are making the decisions and those who are left out

STOP the game after five minutes

- Share your observations with the group
- Invite the participants to share their reflections and feelings
- Notice there are two "cliques" in this model that do not interact.
- One group includes four people and the other five

CITY PARISH WITH LAY MINISTER SITUATION

Our Lady of Mercy Parish is a city parish with long-standing traditions. Changes have come slowly and with much discussion and some anguish. There is a newly founded pastoral council in the parish and one of the most active groups in the parish is the choir.

Lay ministers have been used in the parish with mixed feelings. To make matters worse, one of the lay ministers of communion attracted attention because of "irreverent" attire while on the altar, (jogging shorts).

This caused some of the members of the choir to complain to the pastor about such irreverence for a minister of holy communion. The lay minister, when confronted with this, became indignant and threatened to withhold a sizeable contribution and reveal some past indiscretions heard about the choir if not issued an apology.

Both sides are gathering a following in the parish and it looks like a fight will ensue if something is not done.

You have come to a special meeting of the staff and lay leaders to settle this matter. Spend a moment thinking up solutions and then solve it!

OBSERVER
- Be sure people talk only to those they are connected to by lines
- Pay attention to how people interact rather than the subject matter
- Notice which people talk and which are silent and why
- Notice those who are making the decisions and those who are left out

STOP the game after five minutes

- Share your observations with the group
- Invite the participants to share their reflections and feelings

1-F

LEADERSHIP FLOW

In trying to accomplish a task, solve a problem or create a new project, four types of leadership are necessary. These include *Dreamers*, *Goal-setters*, *Action-takers* and *Harmonizers*. Identifying which of these is your strength, as well as the strengths of those around you will help accomplish the task. Think of a recent situation you were part of that moved from a dream into an action. It could be a small task, like planning a parish social or liturgy, or a large task, such as planning a Lenten program or establishing parish small communities of faith.

1. Identify the task: _____

2. On the diagram below name the people in each of the four areas that helped move the task toward completion:
   A. Dreamers (Who led the visioning or dreaming stage?)
   B. Goal-setters (Who led the group in focusing the dream into goals?)
   C. Action-takers (Who led the group in putting the plan into action?)
   D. Harmonizers (Who helped the group feel good about their work?)

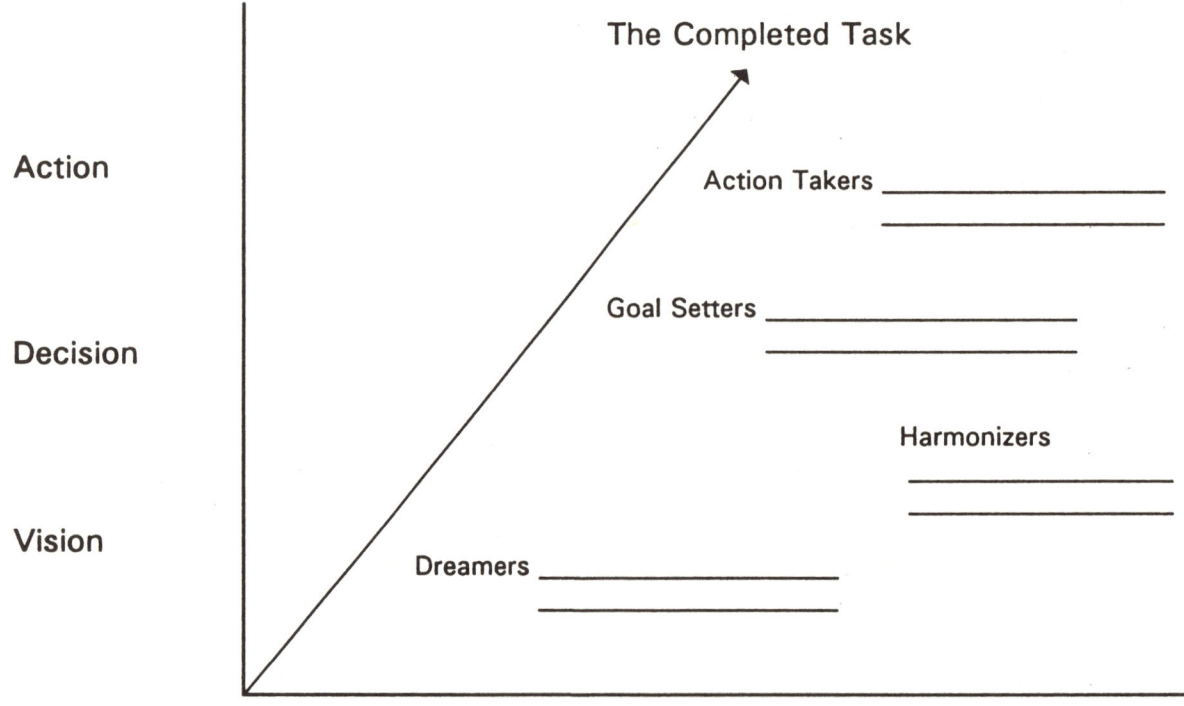

3. What part did *you* play? _____ Was this the best place for you or would you have been more effective in another area?

4. What implication does this have for your ministry or for tasks that lie ahead?

MANAGING STRUCTURES

1-G

My Vision For The Parish: Describe briefly your hopes and dreams for the parish, its liturgies, sense of community, leadership style, formation and outreach.

The Present Structure of the Parish: In the space below (or on the other side if you need more room) draw a diagram of the way the parish is now structured, including pastor, staff, council, groups and ministries. This should be a description of how it *actually* operates, not as it looks in theory. Be creative in making the various individuals and groups larger or smaller depending on their position or influence. Connect individuals and groups together by lines if there is any connection or leave them floating if they are not connected. After drawing the diagram, look at how it helps or hinders the realization of your dream or vision for the parish. Share the results with others for their reactions.

WORK SHEET FOR MANAGING STRUCTURES

1-H

This work sheet is helpful in clarifying what groups and ministries are related and how each contributes to the purpose of that area of parish life. The staff, lay leaders and volunteers responsible for each area of the parish complete the sheet and then pass it around to the various groups and organizations they have listed in order to obtain their reaction and input. The result is a clearer picture of the make-up of that area of the parish, identifying areas of overlap and suggesting avenues for greater sharing and interaction.

AREA OF PARISH LIFE: (Such as Worship, Community, Education, etc.)

_____

PURPOSE OF THIS AREA: (Brief description of what this area should accomplish or provide.)

_____

_____

_____

GROUP/MINISTRY/PROGRAM	PURPOSE OF THIS GROUP OR MINISTRY
1.	
2.	
3.	
4.	
5.	
6.	
7.	
8.	
9.	
10.	
11.	
12.	
13.	

MANAGING STAFF AND COUNCIL MEETINGS

PROCEDURE:

1. If used for a staff meeting, the agenda sheet is passed around to the members beforehand or is made available at the beginning of the meeting. [Work Sheet **1-J1**.] If used for a council meeting, the agenda is prepared beforehand by the executive or agenda committee. [Work Sheet **1-J2**.]

2. In preparing the staff agenda, members add items to the sheet, putting down the topic, their names, and a check in the appropriate column. These columns may differ according to the parish, but in general, they are as follows:

    A. **Informational items**: These might include announcements, people who are sick, information on meetings, dates, etc. They can be handled easily and quickly.

    B. **Decision items**: These are items that have been talked about before and people have been thinking about, but some decision must be reached.

    C. **Feedback items**: These items have to do with existing programs, projects or the way someone is coming across. In an environment of trust, this is the time to air gripes, feelings, positive strokes, etc.

    D. **Planning items**: These items require some thinking by the staff both during the meeting and afterwards. They might be immediate planning for an upcoming event, or more long-range issues. If the planning item needs lengthy discussion, then time is set aside at a future meeting to deal with the issue.

    E. **New business items**: These are new items that people want to mention to get others thinking prior to the next meeting. They come at the end of the meeting as time permits.

3. After all staff members have a chance to put down their agenda items at the beginning of the meeting, the person chairing the meeting (usually this rotates each meeting) takes all the items checked, in the order they were written. Once all these items are dealt with, the chairperson moves on to the second column, and so forth, until the agenda sheet is covered or time is expired. Items not covered in the staff meeting are put at the top of the column for the next meeting. As each item is considered, the chairperson makes any necessary notes in the right hand column. Once the meeting is over, the agenda sheet is copied and distributed. This sheet serves as the minutes of the meeting for future reference.

4. In running council meetings, the same procedure is followed, although the agenda is usually prepared in advance by an executive or agenda committee. The meeting is led by the appointed chairperson or co-chairs. A secretary is responsible for taking notes and more formal minutes are prepared for distribution following the meeting.

1-J1

AGENDA FOR PARISH STAFF MEETING

CHAIRPERSON _____ **DATE** _____

    A. Prayer: Leader _____
    B. Sharing of personal reactions or experiences since the last meeting. (10 minutes)
    C. Agenda items taken according to each category in turn.
    D. Summary of results at the end of the meeting.
    E. Evaluation of the meeting and interaction.

Agenda Item	Member	I	D	F	P	N	Notes
1.							
2.							
3.							
4.							
5.							
6.							
7.							
8.							
9.							
10.							
11.							
12.							
13.							
14.							
15.							
16.							
17.							
18.							
19.							
20.							

(Code [See below])

Code Description:
    I = Information: Announcements, meeting dates, events. (No discussion necessary.)
    D = Decision: Items that have been discussed but now need a decision.
    F = Feedback: Affirming or giving reactions to an existing program, event, ministry, etc.
    P = Planning: Needs discussion about planning an upcoming event, issue, problem, etc.
    N = New Business: New issues, usually to be handled later but included as time permits.

1-J2

AGENDA FOR PASTORAL COUNCIL MEETING

DATE _____

A. Prayer: Leader _____
B. Sharing of personal reactions or experiences since the last meeting. (10 minutes)
C. Reaction to reports or minutes. (Received and read beforehand). (10 minutes)
D. Agenda items taken according to each category in turn.
E. Summary of results at the end of the meeting.
F. Evaluation of the meeting and interaction.

Agenda Item	Presenter	I	D	F	P	N	Notes
1.							
2.							
3.							
4.							
5.							
6.							
7.							
8.							
9.							
10.							
11.							
12.							
13.							
14.							
15.							
16.							
17.							
18.							
19.							
20.							

Columns I, D, F, P, N are headed "Code (See Below)".

Code Description:
- I = Information: Announcements, meeting dates, events. (No discussion necessary.)
- D = Decision: Items that have been discussed but now need a decision.
- F = Feedback: Affirming or giving reactions to an existing program, event, ministry, etc.
- P = Planning : Needs discussion about planning an upcoming event, issue, problem, etc.
- N = New Business: New issues, usually to be handled later but included as time permits.

1-K

FIVE FACTORS OF MOTIVATION

Helping people feel good about what they are doing in the parish, either as a paid staff member or as a volunteer depends upon these five motivators. This work sheet has two parts.

1. Think of a task or ministry in which you served as a participant but not a leader or organizer. What score would you give to each of the five motivators, from one to nine, that best describes your experience?

2. Think of a task or ministry for which you are responsible as a leader or organizer. What score would you give yourself as to the way you help motivate others in this task or ministry?

Compare the results of these two reflections with others in the same situation.

SCORE

```
|----|----|----|----|----|----|----|----|
1    2    3    4    5    6    7    8    9
Poor      Fair      Average   Good      Excellent
```

____ ____ 1. A sense of achievement and success in the work.

____ ____ 2. An experience of challenge and invitation to try out new methods and approaches.

____ ____ 3. An increase of responsibility and less supervision over time.

____ ____ 4. Appropriate recognition and affirmation for work completed.

____ ____ 5. An opportunity for personal growth and spiritual development.

MOTIVATIONS FOR MINISTRY

Reflect on an area of ministry in which you are now involved. Read through the following list of motivational elements related to pastoral ministry. Place a plus (+) in front of the items that you now experience in this ministry. Place a minus (-) in front of the items that you feel are lacking. Share with others in your ministry how those items that are lacking might be addressed in the near future.

In this ministry I feel that:

_____ 1. I am responding to a call rather than doing this work out of obligation.

_____ 2. This work is related to a larger vision of what the church is all about.

_____ 3. I have a chance to interact with others who are involved in similar work to share ideas and experiences.

_____ 4. I have had the opportunity to grow in my faith and prayer life as a result of this work.

_____ 5. I have been given sufficient training and instruction to do this work well.

_____ 6. Money and other resources are available to me if I want to try out a new and creative way of doing this work.

_____ 7. I am given enough affirmation and recognition for the contribution of my time and talents.

_____ 8. There are plenty of occasions for socializing and having fun with others involved in this ministry.

_____ 9. I am not coerced into giving more time than I am able or willing to give, or made to feel guilty if I don't give more of my time.

_____ 10. The meetings and planning sessions associated with this work are productive and enjoyable.

_____ 11. There are people who act as mentors and role models. They help me better understand how to do this work well.

_____ 12. If I have new ideas and suggestions about doing this work, they are listened to and taken seriously.

_____ 13. I have a part to play in the planning, decision-making and direction this work is going.

_____ 14. I enjoy what I am doing and want to keep doing it in the future.

1-M

THE POSITIVE USE OF POWER

The negative side of power is coercive, forcing people to do something against their will. The positive side of power is empowering, helping individuals and groups to move beyond constraints and limits in order to achieve something new. It includes the power to heal, to forgive, to challenge, to nourish.

In order to practice the positive side of power, think of a ministry that has been going on for some time. Examples might include R.C.I.A., youth ministry, the annual festival or refreshments after Mass. Name the ministry and fill in the appropriate information. Then share it with others in the same ministry to see what their reactions might be. This sheet can also be filled out as a group experience for people involved in the same ministry to see how the positive aspects of power are utilized.

1. Area of Ministry: _____

2. List the talents or gifts needed to maintain this ministry and the people who have these gifts.

    Talents and Gifts Needed   *Names of Persons with these Gifts*

    _____   _____
    _____   _____
    _____   _____
    _____   _____

    (Sometimes the positive side of power fails because people with the gifts are not called forward.)

3. What structures, traditions or set patterns are necessary to keep this ministry going? What, if anything, is missing? (Sometimes the positive side of power fails because structures, traditions or patterns are not established to keep this ministry operating.)

    _____
    _____
    _____
    _____

4. What abuses of power or misuse of authority are present in this ministry? How could these abuses be corrected? (Sometimes the positive side of power fails because abuses are not recognized and confronted.)

    _____
    _____
    _____
    _____

Adapted from <u>The Emerging Laity</u> by James D. Whitehead and Evelyn Eaton Whitehead, NY: Doubleday, 1986 (pg. 111-114).

MANAGING THE IMAGE

Process:

PART ONE:

1. Give each person two index cards. On one index card, ask people to write down, in a word or phrase, how they would describe the image *they* have of their own leadership group, whether it is the staff, council, commission or committee.

2. On the second index card, ask people to write down what they think the *parishioners'* image of this group might be.

3. First, have people share their *own* image words or phrases. List these on a large piece of paper or board.

4. Then ask for the word or phrase that describes the *parishioners'* image of their group. List these as well.

5. Discuss the two lists as a group, noting differences and similarities.

PART TWO:

1. Break into groups of three and discuss what is happening *now* that helps create a positive image. Ask the small groups to list other options for improving the image of each of the leadership groups in the parish, or of the parish as a whole.

2. Each small group is to choose one option to present to the large group, along with ideas for possible implementation.

3. The small groups return to the large group to share the results of their discussion. The leaders make plans as to how to manage the image of the various leadership groups in the parish.

AN EXERCISE IN IMAGE BUILDING

This exercise is best done in groups of four or five persons. Give each small group several large sheets of paper and a few wide felt markers of different colors. Ask them to return to the large group in fifteen minutes.

Situation:

You have been put in charge of planning the 10:00 a.m. Sunday Mass that takes place in the school gym. It was originally a place that provided flexibility in the liturgy, but Mass attendance has fallen off recently. What can be done to restore the former spirit and enthusiasm and make it more attractive to the parishioners?

Task:

1. Come up with a one-liner as an image statement to grab the people.

2. Draw a logo or banner for the Mass.

3. Create a new tradition for the ritual, whether a song, entrance rite, ending, etc.

4. Think of a creative way to get the word out to the whole parish that this Mass is here to stay. Think of how to make a mark in the parish.

5. Figure out how people are going to get turned on and enjoy this Mass more. Be creative, use symbols, put this gym Mass back on the map! Realize, however, that it is still part of the parish as a whole so you have to stay within reasonable bounds.

2 | COLLABORATION

INTRODUCTION

Holy Family Parish has started a tradition of joint meetings between the pastoral staff and council. These meetings occur four times a year, focusing on prayer, planning and goal-setting. One of these meetings has become a special event for this group. Its purpose is to plan the appreciation evening for the volunteers. The council and staff take responsibility for planning this yearly event to show their gratitude to the volunteers, without whom the parish goals would never be accomplished. This year the number of volunteers has doubled in size. Their generosity has fostered a holy, caring, and vibrant spirit both within the parish community and the surrounding neighborhood.

Tonight is the planning meeting for this event. The room is filled with energy as the parish leaders gather not only to work together but to enjoy each other's company. The meeting begins with a short prayer, followed by a light dinner. A brainstorming exercise is then used to explore ideas for the event's theme.

Specific responsibilities for carrying out this event have alternated between the two leadership groups. The council chairperson reminds the pastoral staff that this year the planning of the dinner menu and baking desserts are their responsibility. Father Kevin is looking forward to making his chocolate cream puffs, a favorite of many parishioners. The pastoral council is responsible for preparing the thanksgiving prayer service, sending out the invitations and welcoming everyone as they arrive.

Working together and enjoying this collaboration is a new experience for these two leadership groups. Three years ago they hired a facilitator to help them through a difficult time. Clarifying their roles, sharing dreams for the parish, creating a common vision and establishing goals helped them experience and understand the art of *collaboration*. Although struggling at times, they have continued to work together. Turf battles are now settled. They find collaborating with each other generates more creative energy and produces great results.

WHAT IS COLLABORATION?

Collaboration is the art of working well together. People not only provide support and affirmation, but challenge one another to quality ministry. They become co-workers. This is a high ideal that is sometimes held up as the expected way of operating, yet collaboration only goes so far. Team ministry and partnership take collaboration one step further and move into the realm of mutuality and equality. Practice and hard work along with an investment of time, energy and commitment are required.

When group members enter into a team ministry or partnership, they commit themselves to a deeper sense of ownership. A feeling of camaraderie and interdependence develops. Partnership requires meeting on a regular basis and setting aside time for team-building. It demands that the group clarify the meaning of collaboration and mutuality. Work Sheets **2-A** and **2-B** help facilitate this process.

Many staffs have developed a tradition of getting away from the work place once or twice a year for team-building. They spend time sharing individual dreams and expectations for ministry. The group articulates a common vision and establishes goals to move the vision closer to reality. They identify gifts that group members bring to the ministries (Work Sheet **2-C**) and how to use them more effectively. Staffs that operate collaboratively evaluate progress at the end of the year. They discuss how close they have come to achieving their goals and plan strategies for the coming year. (See work sheets in Chapters Six, Seven and Eight.)

A REFLECTION EXERCISE

As groups work toward achieving a sense of partnership and mutuality, they go through several stages of growth. Handout **2-D** identifies the stages and feelings members experience along the way. It provides ideas to help a group move through the stages of development. The handout assists in integrating new members.

Any changes in the composition of the group demands reverting back to earlier stages of growth.

After reading the Stages of Community Groups, spend time reflecting on your personal experience. As a member of a group, in what stage do you now find yourself operating? Based on your perception, where is the group, as a whole, operating? This process will help the members of the group discover similarities and differences in their perceptions of the group. After sharing with one another, the group has a better chance of achieving consensus about where it would like to be. Asking the questions, "What's preventing the group from getting there?" and "What can be done to reach the ideal?" will encourage more dialogue among group members.

Collaboration can be an enriching group experience, as was the case with the staff and council at the beginning of the chapter. When other parishioners experience this group dynamic they, too, want to be part of the positive experience. Committees increase in membership. People enjoy interacting with one another. Tasks are accomplished.

A good model of collaboration is an attractive tool for developing greater ownership among the people. Several exercises throughout this book provide suggestions for fostering collaboration and partnership. Invite groups and individuals to use these activities. Efforts to enable and empower others will motivate them to accept greater responsibility for the parish. By sharing their gifts and talents they participate in shaping parish life and operation.

COSTS AND BENEFITS OF PARTNERSHIP

Although team ministry and partnership are seen by some as ideal ways of working together, they sometimes lead to burnout. There are extra demands and pressures placed on people by these models. Group members are expected to attend meetings in order to share in the planning and evaluating of various programs. They are expected to support and, at times, share in the implementation of ministries other than their own. Giving up a personal idea or goal and creating something different with colleagues. The call to adapt and to be flexible produces anxiety for some members, especially if an individual has a personal need for order and control. With all the problems and conflicts this method incurs why is it considered the ideal?

Partnership gives people a chance to share in the wisdom of others. They move through the process of give and take. By generating new ideas, parishioners' needs are met more effectively. Unleashing a group's energy in this form of interaction creates new realities. The interdependent dynamic that takes place between members goes beyond accomplishing a task. Friendships may develop. New insights are acquired. People have a sense of accomplishment and pride in the outcome. Marvelous programs, good feelings, and success stories become part of the parish history. All this and more happens by saying, "YES," to the challenge of collaboration and partnership.

Work Sheet **2-E** offers a reflection on the costs and benefits of partnership. It challenges people to move beyond collaboration, into the realm of mutuality and equality. Other exercises found on Work Sheets **2-F** through **2-K** help groups critique how well they are working in a collaborative model. Case studies, **2-L1**, **2-L2**, **2-M1**, and **2-M2** are opportunities for practicing the art of collaboration using fictitious situations. As group members utilize the information gained from these reflections they will be in a better position to decide whether or not a more collaborative style is the right choice for them.

CONCLUSION

Working together with people who are committed to share their talents for the benefit of others is a gift in itself. Parishes are blessed with professional staff members and volunteers who accept responsibility for ministering to the People of God. Calling forth gifts and encouraging people to use these gifts in collaborative ministry is worth far more than accomplishing everything alone. Jesus always invited others to come and share in his ministry. His was a collaborative style. We have much to learn from his example.

ADDITIONAL RESOURCES

Ferder, Fran & John Heagle, *Partnership: Women & Men In Ministry*. Notre Dame, IN: Ave Maria Press. 1989.

Pierce, Carol and Bill Page, *A Male/Female Continuum: Paths to Colleagueship*. New Hampshire: A New Dynamics Publication. 1990.

Ramey, David A. *Empowering Leaders*. Kansas City, MO: Sheed & Ward. 1991.

Reddy, W. Brendan, *Intervention Skills: Process Consultation for Small Groups and Teams*. San Diego, CA: Pfeiffer & Co. 1994.

Sofield, Loughlan & Donald H. Kuhn, *The Collaborative Leader, Listening to the Wisdom of God's People*. Notre Dame, IN: Ave Maria Press. 1995.

Stevens, R. Paul & Phil Collins, *The Equipping Pastor*. New York: An Alban Institute Publication. 1993.

Weisbord, Marvin R. and others, *Discovering Common Ground*. San Francisco: Berrett-Kohler. 1992.

2-A

COLLABORATION
(Personal Reflection Sheet)

1. Draw an image (picture of an object) that describes your meaning of *collaboration.*

2. In the space to the left of the line, list ten words that your image suggests.

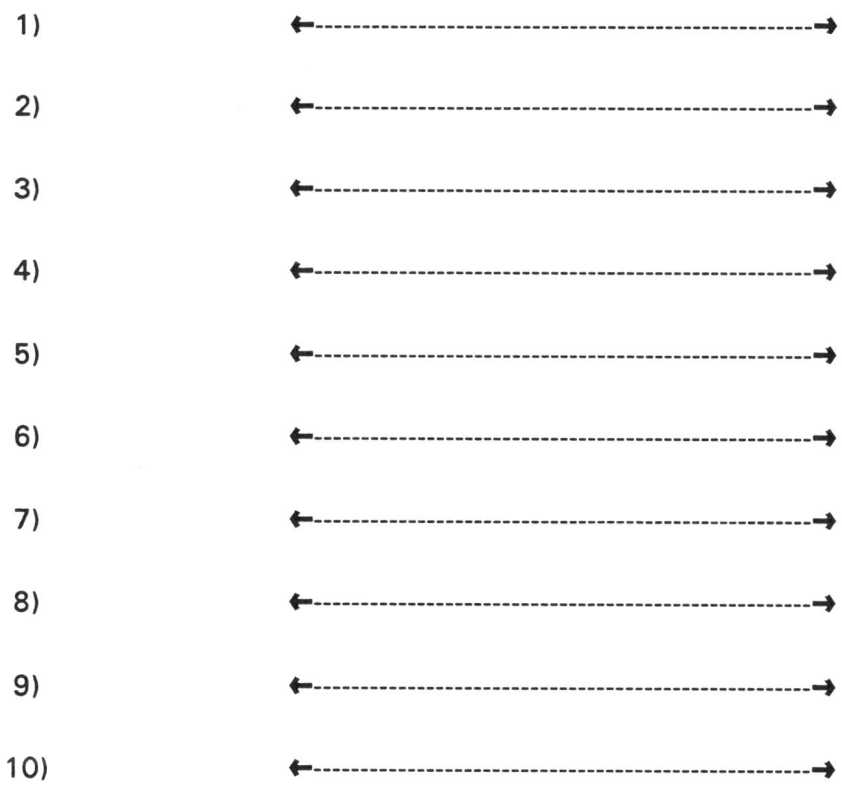

   1) ←--→

   2) ←--→

   3) ←--→

   4) ←--→

   5) ←--→

   6) ←--→

   7) ←--→

   8) ←--→

   9) ←--→

   10) ←--→

3. At the right of each line, list words that are the opposite of the ones already listed.

4. Using each line as a continuum, put an "X" at the spot that best describes your experience of the group. (Staff, council, school board, faculty, ministry group, etc.)

5. Using the same continuum, put an "O" at the spot that best describes where you would **like** the group to be.

6. Share your image and the marks on the continuum lines with one or two others.

MUTUALITY

2-B

Individuals may have varying concepts of mutuality. This exercise will help participants: a) identify times when they experienced mutuality within the group, and b) reflect on what more needs to be done to foster mutuality. By sharing responses, group members will come to a better understanding of mutuality.

REFLECTIONS

What are we doing *now* to foster mutuality?	What *more* needs to be done to foster greater mutuality?

IDENTIFYING GIFTS

2-C

In order to foster the spirit of collaboration, group members support and complement each other's gifts and limitations. Identifying these characteristics helps a group recognize strengths and areas of need. As a group member: a) list your personal strengths and limitations, b) identify three other group members and list the gifts they bring to the group. Share your reflections with other group members. Rejoice in the uncovered gifts. Become aware of areas of need and how members can compensate for what is lacking in others.

Recognizing MY Gifts . . .	Recognizing MY Limitations . . .

Three gifts I bring to the group are:

1. _____
2. _____
3. _____

Three limitations or areas of need I bring to the group are:

1. _____
2. _____
3. _____

Recognizing the Gifts of Group Members

Insert the names of three group members.

The gifts _____ brings to the group are . . .
      (Name)

The gifts _____ brings to the group are . . .
      (Name)

The gifts _____ brings to the group are . . .
      (Name)

STAGES OF COMMUNITY GROUPS

STAGE	PREDOMINANT FEELING	HOW THE FEELING IS EXPRESSED	WHAT CAN YOU DO
1. Orientation	Insecurity	Talking Getting clarity Silence Questioning whether this group meets my needs	Clarify norms, expectations, etc.
2. Inclusion	Fear of exclusion	Do I belong? Will I be accepted? Am I different? Fear of doing something that will get me rejected	Find ways of including everyone Encourage asking questions
3. Control	Competitiveness	How can I be important in this group? Who is most important? Why?	Focus on the unique value of each person Decrease differences Focus on commonality
4. Conflict	Tension	Fight Nonattendance Regression Denial of the problem	Raise the conflict issue and deal with it
5. Cohesion	Relaxation	Lots of interaction Concern for one another Accomplishment of tasks	Make sure the group is moving toward its purpose
6. Faith Sharing	Peacefulness	Honest sharing Trust	Make sure people feel comfortable
7. Intimacy	Ambivalence	How close do I want to get to these people? Approach, avoidance	Discover a comfortable level without feeling guilty
8. Termination	Avoidance	Attempt to avoid the end	Deal with your feelings

Hammett, Rosine, & Loughlan Sofield, *Inside Christian Community*. (The Jesuit Educational Center for Human Development, NY: LeJacq Publ., 1981.) p.14

2-E

PARTNERSHIP

List the benefits and costs of working in partnership with others. Share these reflections with other members in the group.

BENEFITS	COSTS

Following the above exercise, take some quiet time to answer the next two questions. If you wish, share these responses with the group.

REFLECTION

1. What is one change in myself that I am willing to work on to foster mutuality?

2. What is one strategy for mutuality I can implement with my staff and/or ministry group over the next six months?

REFLECTION ON PARTNERSHIP

Groups and individuals say they are committed to working in a partnership mode. The reality does not always match the rhetoric. Reflect on your situations and rate the dynamics of the group. Share the results with others.

From this reflection, what can help or hinder a greater commitment to partnership?

1	2	3	4	5
Poor	Fair	Average	Good	Excellent

1. How do you rate the present level of partnership in your work situation? ____

2. How do you rate your own leadership style in providing a partnership climate? ____

3. How do you rate the people you work with and how they respond to their role as being partners? ____

4. How do you rate the environment of your place of ministry for personal sharing and interaction? ____

5. How do you rate the spirit and motivation of the group you work with? ____

From this reflection, list two things that help and two things that get in the way of a greater commitment to partnership.

HELPS	HINDRANCES

SHARING WISDOM

To empower a group, the leader should provide an environment that is conducive to engaging everyone. How well does your group share the wisdom of its members? Put a plus (+) in front of each item you feel are strengths in your group dynamics. Put a minus (-) in front of each item that you feel is weak and needs to be improved. Share your comments with other group members. Affirm the strengths. Give suggestions to improve the areas of need.

1. Allow people to be true to their own thoughts and feelings

2. Give them the opportunity to think through their thoughts and feelings

3. Help people feel valued within the group

4. Allow each person adequate time to share his/her wisdom

5. Seek information and wisdom from hesitant people

6. Restore the wisdom that was not picked up by the group

7. Curtail the talkers from dominating the conversation

8. Check out and express group feelings of tension, weariness, confusion and joy

9. Provide a sense of order and discipline as the group seeks to arrive at a consensus

10. Summarize and synthesize group decisions and plans of action

11. Help the group achieve a sense of closure on issues

12. Confront inappropriate behavior kindly, clearly and consistently

Adapted from Sharing Wisdom by Mary Benet McKinney, OSB, Allen, TX: Tabor Press, © 1987.

"SANE" APPROACH TO PARTNERSHIP

Shifting to a *partnership* mode means different things to different people. To help clarify levels of understanding, each member is asked to identify personal needs, expectations and boundaries for working in this model. After completing the first section of the work sheet, share these reflections with other group members. Listen well. Alternative ways of operating may become clear. List them, then negotiate the specifics. This exercise clarifies group members' behavior and can prevent misunderstandings and conflicts in the future.

1. **STATE:** (These are my needs, expectations and boundaries related to partnership.)

    NEEDS:

    EXPECTATIONS:

    BOUNDARIES:

Discuss the above with one or more group members.

2. **ALTERNATIVES:** (In light of our discussion what alternatives do we have?)

3. **NEGOTIATE:** (What alternatives would be best if we choose to work in partnership?)

4. **EVALUATE:** (Assess progress after a period of time.)

HELPS FOR IMPROVING COLLABORATIVE MINISTRY

How do you rate your group on the following elements? Using the scale where
Excellent = 5   Good = 4   Mixed Feelings = 3   Fair = 2   Poor = 1,
put the appropriate number in front of each item. Share the reasons for such a ranking with other group members. Affirm the strengths. Give suggestions for improving the areas of need.

The degree to which our group:

_____   1. Has a compelling vision or direction

_____   2. Has quality meeting times together, uses limits well

_____   3. Creates a conducive environment for personal sharing

_____   4. Takes risks for faith sharing and personal disclosure

_____   5. Rotates chairperson's role, including both men and women

_____   6. Has facilitating leadership that frees the group to be effective

_____   7. Has clear job descriptions for all staff members including the priests

_____   8. Provides updating for entire staff/group attendance at workshops

_____   9. Is visible as a group at liturgies and activities

_____ 10. Backs up one another during crises

_____ 11. Faces and seeks to manage interpersonal conflicts

_____ 12. Talks out varying concepts of intimacy, power, authority

_____ 13. Takes time to integrate new members into the group

_____ 14. Works at providing job security for all members

_____ 15. Establishes an evaluation process for the group and individual members

GROUP DYNAMICS

Observing group dynamics provides insight into how well a group collaborates. With your own group in mind, rate each of the following elements as you experience it happening among group members. **Agree = 3, Mixed Feelings = 2, Disagree = 1.**

ITEM: **Rating**

1. We spend time together in prayer. _____
2. We spend time together planning. _____
3. We spend time together socializing. _____
4. We care for each group member personally. _____
5. We are concerned about each member's area of ministry. _____
6. We have clear job descriptions. _____
7. We use a consensus model for decision-making. _____
8. We manage conflict situations well. _____
9. We accept constructive criticism from one another. _____
10. We affirm each other's strengths. _____
11. We are encouraged to share our gifts and talents. _____
12. There is an equality among all members of the group, including the clergy. _____
13. We have clear evaluation procedures. _____
14. A majority of the parish is aware of our collaborative efforts. _____
15. A majority of the parish is favorable to our collaborative efforts. _____

Compare the results of the rating with other members in your group.

A PARTNERSHIP FANTASY

When trying to operate as partners, people feel the constraints and restrictions of the situation. The following exercise provides an opportunity to fantasize about partnership. Around the frame of the diagram are conditions within which to operate. Given these conditions, indicate how you would operate as a partner. Share the results of your reflections with at least one other person.

WHAT IF . . .

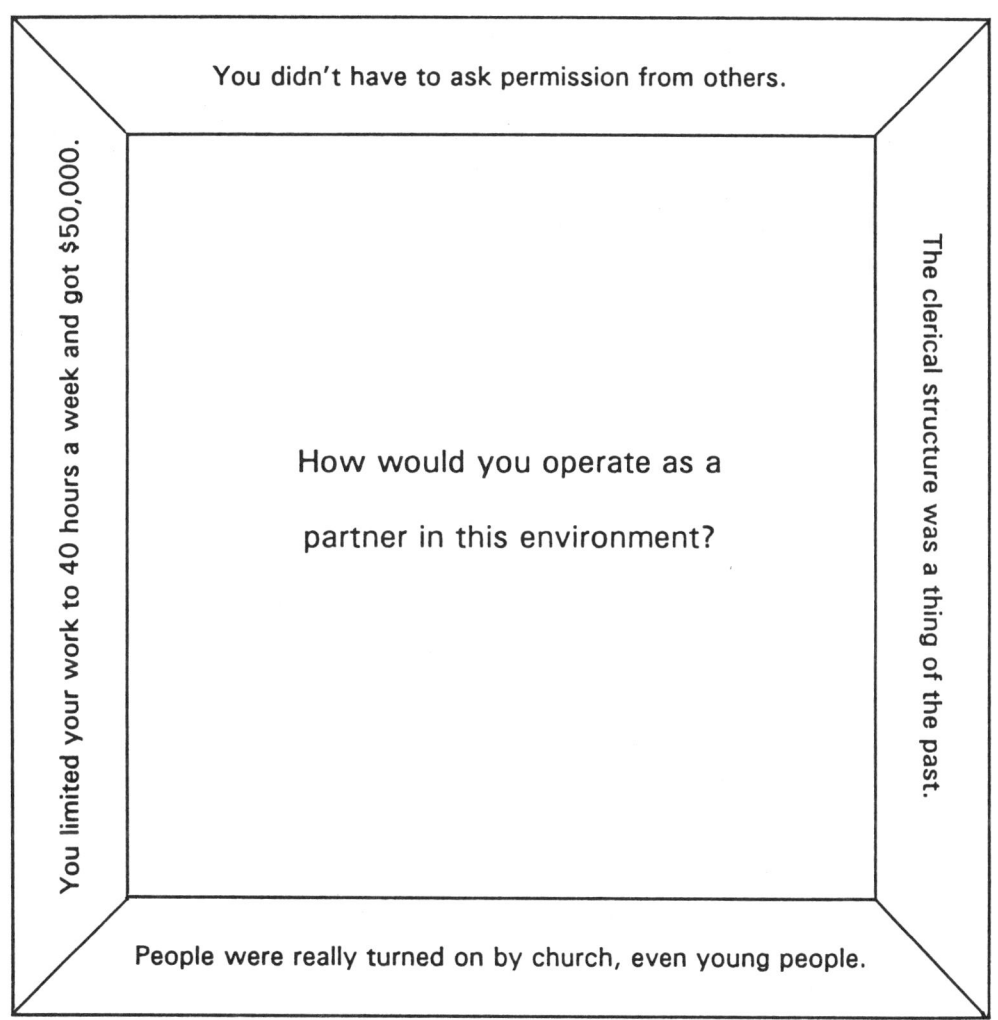

Frame conditions:
- You didn't have to ask permission from others.
- You limited your work to 40 hours a week and got $50,000.
- The clerical structure was a thing of the past.
- People were really turned on by church, even young people.

Center: How would you operate as a partner in this environment?

What insights does this reflection provide for your present situation and area of ministry?

2-L1

COLLABORATION: SOME WIN ...

The Pastoral Associate

Instructions: This role-play is done in conjunction with 2-L2. Read over your character part and then take up where the script leaves off. This role-play can be done in the **best** or the **worse** possible way. Decide how you will do it before you begin. **Time limit: 7 minutes**.

After completing the role-play identify issues that either helped or hindered collaboration. How do these issues relate to your own situation?

Description:
Your name is Sr. Mary Hampton and at the age of 37 you are the pastoral associate of the parish. (Your Myers-Briggs profile is INFJ.) You were hired last year to be in charge of pastoral care in this parish of 1100 families.

Although you had some misgivings at the beginning because the job description was so vague, you have fallen in love with the place during your short stay. The Eucharistic ministers and the outreach committee with whom you work are marvelous people. They were hungry for a staff person with whom they could communicate and share ideas.

You have been able to form a women's group that meets every week. The discussions are lively and the level of sharing and support amazing, given the few months this group has been together.

All would be roses in the parish were it not for the pastor. He is such a lovable guy, but he is so dense. He thinks he knows his people because he stands in the back of the church for all the Masses and greets them, but some of the people resent his condescending, "fatherly" manner.

You have tried to challenge him in his sexist language, especially in his homilies, but it's obvious you are not making much progress. He's like a big teddy bear, lots of good will, but not very organized or intuitive.

You had thought about giving up. It's getting to be too much strain to bridge the gap between the pastor and people, but then you reconsidered. The people are so great and they are responding to you well. Harry, the pastor, does have his good points. Maybe one more year and then you can decide to stay or leave.

You are glad Harry asked you to come see him today. It would be a good time to tell him the news that you have decided to stay for another year.

You have just walked into his office and are sitting down in the chair. Too bad his desk is so big, it creates a distance between both of you. He looks very tired. You wonder what's bothering him.

2-L2

COLLABORATION: SOME WIN ...

The Pastor

Instructions: This role-play is done in conjunction with 2-L1. Read over your character part and then take up where the script leaves off. This role-play can be done in the **best** or the **worse** possible way. Decide how you will do it before you begin. **Time limit: 7 minutes.**

After completing the role-play identify issues that either helped or hindered collaboration. How do these issues relate to your own situation?

Description:
Your name is Fr. Harry Wallace and at the age of 52 you are the pastor of the parish. (Your Myers-Briggs profile is ESFP.) You pride yourself in getting to know almost all 1100 families of the parish in the five years you have been pastor. Your reputation for friendliness and openness goes before you. In short, you are loved by your people.

Last year you began to realize that you could not keep up with the demands for pastoral care, so you hired Sr. Mary Hampton to be the Pastoral Associate. You wanted her to visit the shut-ins, organize the ministers of Communion, take care of the needy families, etc. It was a new job so she could let it develop as she got more into it.

Now, a year later, you are not so sure it was a good idea. Not only is she taking care of pastoral visiting and social needs -- and she does an excellent job at it -- she has also gotten off on the women's issue tangent.

Her strong stands are causing problems with your staff and lay leaders. Last month it carried into the parish as well. She put a notice in the bulletin about the formation of a woman's group. This is all fine and well, but she also indicated that the subject of the first meeting would be the discussion of a national newspaper ad signed by pro-abortionists. You got a lot of phone calls on that one!

She's also getting after you about using men and "he" in your homilies. You know your people and you know that emphasizing he/she will only get them distracted and upset. It's getting out of hand.

In light of all this you have come to the decision not to renew her contract for the coming year. You'll give her good references, no hard feelings, but she just doesn't fit in here.

She is just now coming into your office and is settling down in the chair on the other side of your desk. You're a bit nervous about this but determined, nonetheless.

CASE STUDY ON COLLABORATION

Instructions: Read the case study out loud. Assign rolls to different members for reading: Narrator, Pastor, Director of Religious Education, Principal. You have been asked to facilitate the fallout of this meeting. After listening to the scenario, you have two tasks. First, identify the issues and areas of conflict. Second, develop a process that enables this group to act more collaboratively. (If there are a number of small groups working on this task, ask them to come together and share their insights in the large group.) "Solutions" to the case study can be applied to actual situations related to group dynamics.

Narrator: Background: Our story deals with the staff of St. Agatha's parish situated on the edge of a changing part of the city. It is still predominately white. The average age of the parishioners is increasing.

Staff: The pastor, in his 50's, an associate fresh from the seminary, an elderly Sister who is principal of the school, a laywoman DRE in her late 30's and the permanent deacon in his late 50's. The deacon's wife usually sits in on the staff meetings and is active in the parish pastoral care program.

The staff interaction has improved over the last year. The pastor is growing more accustomed to the mutual sharing among staff members, and longer prayer time at staff meetings. He is less defensive about his authority position and more open to women as (nearly) equal staff members. The principal is speaking up more at meetings and is discovering her role goes beyond just school matters. The young associate is letting this new experience influence his theories and theologies about parish life. He is learning to accept the parish as it is. The DRE is pleased by the growth of the staff toward a *team* concept. She is happy that more people are taking *ownership* and not letting the pastor be the one to make the final decisions. The deacon and his wife are also happy to see the staff closer together, although they don't have the time to spend on staff projects or go on the occasional staff outings as do the other members. All would have continued growing and developing in a positive direction had it not been for a financial crisis that suddenly came up.

Crises: Last week the pastor received a letter from the city indicating that because of cutbacks in funds the city would no longer be able to rent the parish school annex for their continuing education program. It was this rent money that allowed the parish to maintain the parish school without going into debt. The pastor panicked. He called in his financial advisors and asked them what to do. Closing the school was out of the question. Perhaps other items could be cutback to make up the loss. The obvious place to cut would be the religious education budget. Perhaps it could get along without a secretary and maybe even without a staff person. After all, her salary was three times that of any other person on staff. The pastor protested but he saw the logic in their reasoning.

He went to the next staff meeting with a heavy heart. Perhaps if he brought it up during the prayer, as a petition, it would not cause so much of a problem. During the petitions he prayed:

Pastor: *That we come together in this time of crisis when the school annex will no longer be rented by the city, let us pray to the Lord.*

Narrator: This news fell like a ton of bricks. No other petitions followed. Everyone remained silent and people looked around at each other with confused expressions. This was the first hint they had of any difficulty. After prayer, the DRE asked, as gently as she could:

DRE: *When, Joe, did you hear this news?*

Pastor: *Last week. I thought it was a financial matter that concerned my financial advisors more than the staff. We should spend our time here on spiritual concerns, not temporal ones.*

DRE: *Joe, we are in this together. We want to help each other out in critical times. We want to work as a team and not as separate individuals.*

Narrator: She said this in an even tone, trying to control the anger and confusion she felt. The pastor was reverting back to being *in charge* rather than confiding in the staff. At this point, the principal, becoming worried about her school, spoke up:

Principal: *Father, does this mean that we will have to close the school?*

Pastor: *No, no, Sister, we have worked it out so that nothing in the school budget will be touched. All the men supported the school and the good it is doing for the parish.*

DRE: *Joe, let's get this straight. The school budget stays but what about the religious education budget? Is that what goes?*

Pastor: *Ah, yes. Now that you mention it. The men advised me that perhaps we could cut back on some of the services we offer in religious education. Well, not the services exactly. Perhaps some of the support structures, such as the religious education secretary, and making up for the loss with volunteers.*

Narrator: At this point, the climate of the meeting changed. The DRE's face became red. The young associate who was about to jump to the DRE's defense, held back. He knew he had to stay on the good side of the pastor so he kept his mouth shut. The principal, somewhat embarrassed because the school was secure but the religious education was not, wanted to support the DRE but withdrew from the conflict. The deacon, who had been a trustee of the parish, understood the difficulties the pastor faced in trying to pay the bills. He started to come to the defense of the pastor. One look from his wife made him think twice about speaking up so he remained quiet. The deacon's wife gave supportive looks to the DRE but since she was not really a staff person, kept out of the fray. The pastor, looking somewhat sheepish, suggested that they take some time to think about this matter. Right now time was wasting and there were other items on the agenda. He then went on to the next item; the communal penance service coming up next month. Somehow everyone got through the meeting in one piece. The atmosphere remained tense over the next week. A number of one-to-one conversations took place between staff members, mostly in support of either the pastor or the DRE. The DRE finally decided to make an appointment with the pastor to get the facts.

DRE: *Joe, you realize that I could rally support for my programs by stirring up the religious education teachers and parents and the adults in our discussion series. But this is no way to settle this issue. I joined this staff because I thought we could develop into a team ministry. I had such hopes. Now you have reversed our direction. You have gone back to making the decisions and announcing these to the rest of us on staff. I am not sure I can continue working in this situation. I'm not sure you wouldn't want me to resign. It would take you off the hook.*

Pastor: *Karen, you have done a great job here and have helped all of us grow together as a staff. As you know, it has been difficult for me but I'm learning. What am I supposed to do? I can't let this place go bankrupt.*

Narrator: The meeting was not a pleasant one for either the pastor or the DRE. At the end, the DRE suggested that someone from outside the situation be asked to facilitate the next staff meeting, someone not as emotionally involved in the issue. This was a new approach for the pastor, but in a moment of desperation, he agreed. You have been asked to come to the next staff meeting and help deal with this difficult situation. Identify the issues and describe how you would handle this crisis at the next meeting. You are given a free reign to do whatever you think best. Talk it over among yourselves and come up with your plan of action.

3 | DECISION-MAKING

INTRODUCTION What happens when the school board collects $20,000 for new computers and wants to have them installed immediately? They don't even consider that just last month the parish paid $35,000 for a new school furnace because the school was over budget! Or, what happens when the pastor gets a call from the bishop inquiring about a speaker scheduled for an adult education series in the parish. The bishop informs him that she is not an approved speaker because of her public views on women's ordination. The pastor has not heard of the woman and did not know she was coming. Now the bishop wonders what he, the pastor, is going to do about it!

These kinds of things may never happen in your community, but in some parishes confusion over who makes what decisions has led to some tense moments. How decisions are made, and who makes them, reflects the real style of leadership practiced in a parish. Many difficulties associated with decision-making can be reduced by approaching decisions as a step-by-step process. Here are some ideas for managing decisions before they manage you!

WHAT'S THE ISSUE?

The first step of any decision-making process must include discovering the real issue. Parishes all have their share of people who complain about Mass being too long. It is easy to conclude that these people simply want to get in and out as quickly as possible. They lack spiritual depth. The worship committee concludes that only a shorter Mass would make them happy. Maybe there is another issue. The committee decides to talk to a few of these chronic complainers, and what they learn is amazing. The parish has grown. Getting a good seat at Mass now means coming 20 minutes early. Trying to exit the parking lot is impossible unless you leave right after communion because people for the next Mass are already arriving. Maybe the *real* issue is not fading spirituality, but adjusting the schedule, adding another Mass or even enlarging the worship space. Perhaps the problem is that the homilies do not relate to a person's daily life or that there is no reliable child care. Discover the deeper issue and you treat the "disease and not a symptom." Building a school is a solution. Providing more ways to pass on our faith to our children is an issue. Increasing contributions is a solution. A greater sense of ownership among our people is an issue. Once you have defined the issue, you can be creative in developing solutions and choosing the best.

WHO IS INVOLVED? WHAT ARE THE ROLES?

Once the issue is focused, determine who will be the actual decider. Whether a group or a person, this step is vital in clarifying the roles of everyone involved. People respond to the decision-making process differently depending on whether they are being asked for advice, or being asked to actually make the decision. Naming the decision-making person or group helps everyone else know where they stand in relation to the decision.

Once the decision-makers are named, those who provide information to the deciders are the *consultants*. Consultants might include people who will be effected by the decision, or those with expertise or experience in the area of concern. It must be clear you are asking for ideas and suggestions, not for more decision-makers. Consultation gives people a chance to share their wisdom, to have their voice heard and their opinions valued. Ultimately, including the insights of this group will create a wider sense of ownership.

As the decision-making process continues, it may be determined that the issue has changed and that there are others who should be part of the decision-making. Adjustments may need to be made.

When a decision has finally been reached, the process is not finished. Everyone affected by the decision and all who were consulted must be *informed* about what was decided. Communication is a challenging issue in almost every community. By managing this portion of decision-making you will save many misunderstandings and hard feelings.

C – D – I

1. Discover core Problem/Issue/Need
2. Determine actual deciders

What	Who	When
Consult	Who needs to be consulted?	Before
Decide	Who is *really* deciding?	During
Inform	Who needs to be informed?	After

This method of decision-making, Consulting – Deciding – Informing, or *CDI*, can be used for making all types of decisions. It takes practice to remain faithful to the step-by-step process.

Work Sheet **3-A** outlines this process and can be used to keep these principles in focus. You may want to work through the process question-by-question until it becomes more comfortable.

LEVELS OF DECISION-MAKING

This process sounds quite elaborate if we are talking about what color to make the Advent Program covers or where to set up for a party. Of course, all decisions do not need this degree of communication. Some "detail" decisions can and should be handled by an individual or group responsible for this area. Others need input from many different sources. Deciding the appropriate level can be a great asset as a group tries to move through a packed agenda. Work Sheet **3-B** can help guide this process.

The most basic level of decision-making involves all the little day-to-day things. Examples of *NITTY-GRITTY* decisions might include how to heat up the hot dogs for the parish picnic, what to get the religious education teachers as an appreciation gift and yes, what color to make the Advent Program covers! Nitty-gritty does not mean unimportant but those involved can handle it on their own.

Some decisions simply need a vote of confidence. Again, these *SMALL MATTERS* are not unimportant, but they do not need to hang up a meeting. Small matters might include affirming a staff member's research and choice of location for the annual staff retreat or allowing a particular religious community to speak to the congregation on Mission Sunday. You will know very quickly if an issue can be handled as a small matter or if further discussion is needed. If, in taking a "vote of confidence," there are serious questions or concerns raised then you must move to the next level.

CONSENSUS is an effective tool when strong emotions, questions or concerns are present. The group must be willing to invest time and energy in this type of discussion. Consensus involves listening as well as stating your position. Both are important elements for coming to the best possible decision. If real feelings only come out in the "meeting after the meeting" (often held in the parking lot), consensus has not been achieved. A good group leader or facilitator helps this method work by calling each person to participate in the process. The goal of consensus is that all leave with a sense of ownership no matter what the decision. Everyone can live with it and will give support to the result.

In the discussion to gain consensus there may be other issues that surface. These are often pieces of a bigger picture. You begin to wonder "Why did we open this can of worms?!" Don't get overwhelmed, but recognize you have moved to the next level of decision-making. There is a deeper issue that needs to be acknowledged. *PROBLEM SOLVING* moves beyond the question at hand. It's time to think bigger. Work Sheet **3-C** gives an outline for the problem solving process. The most difficult part of this process is Step 1, stating the need. This takes us back to the beginning of the chapter. Review "What's the issue?" to help focus this step. Use this method to move beyond vested interests and let the creative juices flow.

We now come to the *BIG MATTERS – DISCERNMENT*. These issues, such as building or closing a school or renovating the worship space, deeply effect many people. Leaders must move carefully through a process that involves as much of the community as possible. The goal, with the guidance of the Holy Spirit, is to surface the best possible solution, one that the community owns and supports. Discernment involves the wider community in developing a proposal, reflecting on the strengths and weaknesses, providing opportunities for input and feedback and finally a chance for all to share the fruit of their reflections. Work Sheet **3-D** could be used to gather information from members of the community on whatever issue it is facing. In making a large parish decision, the individual reflections would be gathered and given to a discernment group. This group listens to the Spirit speaking through the many opinions and perspectives. It is the collective wisdom of the community that forms the final result. Work Sheet **3-D** could also be used by a parish staff, council, or other group struggling with an important issue. One simple use of the process can be found on Work Sheet **3-E**. This discernment for council chairs contains the same elements used in parish-wide discernment.

Warning: Finding agreement on what level a particular decision should be made is very subjective. Be attentive to those who may have emotional energy regarding any given decision. Include them in whatever ways possible. This inclusion can help avoid negative repercussions once the decision is implemented.

One idea is to investigate what level members of a group would assign past decisions. Try this exercise: Ask the group to give you five or six decisions that have been made recently. These can be big or small decisions, but the closer they are related to the group the better.

After reviewing the levels of decision-making, ask each person to write down the level they feel is most appropriate for each decision. Get into small groups and see if you can reach consensus as to the most appropriate level. Share these levels in the large group listening to the reasons behind each response. Reflect on how the decision was actually made. What would you do differently in the future?

PRACTICE PRACTICE PRACTICE

As clear as this may all seem, *doing* it can be quite a challenge. A first step is assessing how well you are already doing. Work Sheet **3-F** can be used by a staff, pastoral council, or any group to evaluate its decision-making style and make choices for the future. Once an individual reflects on the decisions from her/his perspective, discussions in small groups and then sharing with the larger group can help all evaluate what is really happening.

As we said in the beginning of this chapter, decision-making reflects a style of leadership. What does your decision-making process reveal? Is it what you would like it to be? Could increasing consultation and informing people of results make your decision-making process more effective? Managed well, decision-making can be a process that unifies and brings new life to any group or community.

ADDITIONAL RESOURCES

Freeman, J. Stephen, ed., *Shaping Our Future, Challenges For The Church In The Twenty-first Century.* Cambridge, MA: Cowley Publications. 1994.

Sweetser, SJ, Thomas P. and Patricia M. Forster, OSF, *Transforming the Parish, Models for the Future.* Kansas City: Sheed & Ward. 1993. pp. 81-103.

3-A

STEP - BY - STEP WITH C - D - I

1) Focus: What is the problem/issue/need?

_____
_____

2) Who is the best person or group to make this decision?

_____
_____
_____

3) **CONSULTING:**

Who needs to be consulted before making this decision? (Who will be affected by outcome? Who has experience, or additional information that may be important?) How will this information be gathered and presented to decision-maker(s)? What is the deadline for gathering this information?

_____
_____
_____
_____
_____

4) **DECIDING:**

Is the person or group chosen to make the decision still the best? What deadline is there for making a decision?

_____
_____
_____
_____

5) **INFORMING:**

Who needs to know the result of this decision before it is implemented? How will this decision be communicated? When will this be completed?

_____
_____
_____
_____

LEVELS OF DECISION-MAKING

Choose the appropriate level considering: number of people involved, emotional level, time available, expenses, authority to make the decision. Discuss views with others involved.

1. **NITTY-GRITTY** - Delegating

    When to use: Decision is about specific details, small issues, limited influence

    How to use: Let those in charge take care of the decisions.
    Allow freedom of work and movement.

2. **SMALL MATTERS** - Voting

    When to use: Issues with little conflicting emotion; need vote of confidence

    How to use: Votes of confidence and support. Help people to "own" the decision - no need to hang up meeting over these matters.
    (BE CAREFUL - if there is strong emotion over an issue, potentially dividing the group, move to the next level of decision-making)

3. **LARGER MATTERS** - Consensus

    When to use: Issue has strong emotions and minority opinion could divide the group or community. Issue needs thought and discussion. Time is available to consider options. Group members are willing to listen to and be influenced by each other.

    How to use: All state views on the issue - silence blocks; **No** vote (or straw vote with no power, to assess attitudes); seek out differences of opinion to explore options; don't give in just to avoid conflict; final decision is acceptable to all - meaning all can "live with it" and support it.

4. **PROBLEM SOLVING** - Finding Creative Alternatives

    When to use: Large issues that need group effort to come up with creative alternatives and choosing the best.

    How to use: State the need. (NOT solutions!)
    Envision the ideal if need is met. List what we are already doing to meet the ideal. Think of **all** the ways of reaching the ideal. Be creative! Select the best way(s). Settle on specifics (what, for whom, when, how often, where, by whom, how much).

5. **BIG MATTERS** - Discernment

    When to use: Issue affects entire parish community and many will have **strong** emotion over outcome of decision.

    How to use: State problem/situation.
    Consult with those involved and develop **possible** solution.
    Take time in prayer and thought and list all reasons **against**.
    Time for prayer and thought on all reasons **for**.
    Eventually, solution will arise as a result. If not, continue process.

3-C

PROBLEM SOLVING PROCESS
Finding Creative Alternatives

Use this process to develop creative solutions to the situation at hand. The first and most important step is identifying the core issue or need. Stay clear of solutions! Once this is clear to all, move ahead with the process.

1. STATE THE NEED: _____

2. ENVISION THE IDEAL: (What would it look like if we completely solved this issue? Be creative!!! This is a time for dreaming.)
   _____
   _____
   _____
   _____

3. WHAT ARE WE ALREADY DOING TO REACH THIS IDEAL?
   _____
   _____
   _____
   _____

4. WHAT MORE COULD BE DONE TO REACH THE IDEAL? (Don't worry about limits here. Dream!)
   _____
   _____
   _____
   _____
   _____

5. SELECT THE **BEST** WAY OF REACHING THE IDEAL: (Given the reality of resources, timelines and other considerations, what can we really do?)
   _____
   _____
   _____

6. ACTION STEPS: (List details to carry out action. This might include: where, when, by whom, for whom, how often, how much, consultation needed, who to inform, other details?)
   _____
   _____
   _____
   _____
   _____

DISCERNMENT WORK SHEET

3-D

Decision To Be Made: _____
_____
_____
_____

Reasons In Favor	Reasons Against
_____	_____
_____	_____
_____	_____
_____	_____
_____	_____
_____	_____
_____	_____
_____	_____
_____	_____
_____	_____
_____	_____
_____	_____
_____	_____
_____	_____

= =

Discernment Card

After prayerful reflection, I suggest that the proposal:_____,
be [please check one]   Accepted_____   Not Accepted_____   because...
(please write in one reason supporting your response):

_____
_____
_____
_____

DISCERNMENT PROCESS FOR COUNCIL CHAIRPERSON(S)

-Prayer (set mood):
   The entire session should be spent in a prayerful atmosphere. Council members ask themselves, "What are we being called to?"

-Individual reflections: (write down answers to the following questions)
   a) The two reasons why I would be effective as council chairperson are...
      The talents I have to offer as a council chairperson are...
   b) The one/two reasons why I would not be a good council chairperson are...
      The things that might get in the way and prevent me from being a good council chairperson are...

-Share reflections with the entire group.
   a) Everyone should share the positive reasons only.
   b) Everyone should share the negative reasons.

-Write down the names of the two people who you feel would be the most effective chairpersons.

-List all the names chosen so everyone can see them

-Check with individuals to see if they are willing to keep their names on the list.

-From this list, write the names of your first and second choices

-Gather the names and add the results. The first choice gets four points and the second choice gets two points.

-The two highest scores are asked to accept the positions of co-chairpersons.

-Acceptance and ratification.

EXPLORING PAST DECISIONS

Name three decisions that have been made in the recent past. For each decision, name the level of decision-making used:

    1- Nitty Gritty,   2- Small Matter,   3- Consensus,   4- Problem Solving,   5- Discernment

Answer questions for each decision, exploring how a decision was handled and what might have been done differently. These can be done individually and then answers shared in groups.

Name Decision:	
Level of decision-making used:	What level should have been used?
Who was Consulted?	Who should have been consulted?
Who Decided?	Was this the best person/group to make decision?
Who was Informed?	Who should have been informed?

Name Decision:	
Level of decision-making used:	What level should have been used?
Who was Consulted?	Who should have been consulted?
Who Decided?	Was this the best person/group to make decision?
Who was Informed?	Who should have been informed?

Name Decision:	
Level of decision-making used:	What level should have been used?
Who was Consulted?	Who should have been consulted?
Who Decided?	Was this the best person/group to make decision?
Who was Informed?	Who should have been informed?

4 | CONFLICT MANAGEMENT

INTRODUCTION Two parishioners who volunteered to coordinate the Adult Formation Committee are planning a six-week series focused on parenting children. The sessions are scheduled to take place in the rectory meeting room on the first and third Tuesday of the month starting in October. The Director of Religious Education, who is the staff liaison with this committee, is confronted by another staff member. It seems that she has used the rectory meeting room for the R.C.I.A. group on Tuesdays for the last three years. What right do they have taking her space? No one checked with her.

Conflict situations arise in a parish as people begin to take ownership of ministries and programs. Scheduling events, implementing dreams, orchestrating a process and making unilateral decisions can be some of the causes of tension and anxiety. An effort should be made to see these conflict situations as opportunities for growth. When this is done, individuals can grow in self-knowledge, uncover struggles and address authority issues. Facing conflicts in a healthy way can also increase performance and ministry effectiveness. The secret to appreciating the value of conflict lies in developing skills for managing the conflict situations.

MANAGING CONFLICT People address conflict management in different ways. Some *AVOID* it, thinking it will go away. This method is fine if the issue is unimportant or the timing is wrong. They need a cooling off period. However, it is inappropriate if the issue is important and will not go away. When emotions build up inside, an unhealthy outburst can occur if the conflict is not managed.

When people choose harmony at all costs they may *ACCOMMODATE* to the will of another. They give up their goal to protect the relationship. This is appropriate if the relationship is tenuous or a person exercises some authority. However, it is inappropriate if the relationship is strong and the people are committed to honest sharing and mutuality.

Another method of conflict management is that of *WIN/LOSE*. Here a person or group settles the conflict with no dialogue. If people do not have the same experience, age, or position this method may be acceptable, or in crisis situations when there is no time for dialogue. It is definitely inappropriate if a group has decided to act collaboratively, or if this will cause future disruptions.

COMPROMISE is best used when parties need room to maneuver or resources and time are limited. Both parties give in some and a middle ground is reached. However, if the solution is watered-down so that it is no longer desirable or people don't go far enough in seeking alternatives, this method would be inappropriate.

The *WIN/WIN* method is by far the best method if time is available and people are committed to mutuality and collaboration. There must also be the desire to take the risks necessary to enter into this level of communication. Learning the skills to foster this method is strongly suggested. Here are some skills that will help.

WIN/WIN SKILLS

Creative active listening is important if someone has a conflict with you. Ask them questions to encourage dialogue. While they are sharing, listen attentively to become aware of the conflict situation they are experiencing. Once the information is out in the open you can begin talking about your perceptions and clear the air.

The conflict situations you remember most are the ones you have with someone else. Use the **"I Statement"** method. Share a **concrete situation** with the other person: "Do you remember this situation occurring?" Describe it. Now share your **feelings** about the situation: "I felt angry, intimi-

CONFLICT MANAGEMENT / 59

dated, etc." Remember to *own* the feelings. Do not use comments like, "You made me feel. . ." Now share your **reaction** and/or **behavior** since the conflict occurred.

If two or more people are involved in the conflict, the **"SANE"** approach works well.

S   Have everyone **STATE** their needs.

A   Discuss **ALTERNATIVES**.

N   **NEGOTIATE** which of the options will be chosen, then choose one.

E   After implementing the option of choice for a short time, **EVALUATE** the situation to see if any changes need to be made or if things are working better.

If no conflicts occur within your group, be suspicious. You may not be investing enough of yourself and collaboration may be a superficial expression of your working together.

PRACTICING SKILLS

Knowing how you react in times of conflict is important. Work Sheets **4-A** and **4-B** are designed to help you identify your conflict management style. Causes of conflict can occur from outside the group as well as from inside. With reflection, Work Sheet **4-C** can help you identify these causes and the resources available to manage them. Work Sheet **4-D** can be used as an aid for describing the conflict and choosing the appropriate skills for managing it.

CASE STUDIES

Knowledge of the skills for conflict management is one thing, choosing the appropriate skills and using them is another story. When a group desires to become more skilled in this area, using current conflict situations can be threatening and emotional. Case studies are a good way for people to practice the appropriate skills and become comfortable in applying them to their real situation. Work Sheets **4-E1** to **4-G2**, provide three case studies for this purpose. Each situation gives two people an opportunity to enter into dialogue with each other and role-play a conflict situation using the appropriate skills. People may appreciate getting feedback from an observer on how well they are applying the skills, as well as learning their areas of weakness. The feedback process can be facilitated by using Work Sheet **4-H** with these exercises.

Work Sheets **4-I** to **4-L** provide four case studies to be used as group exercises. These case studies have two steps:

1) Volunteers create the scenario applying conflict management skills and then act it out. When the role-play is over discuss issues arising and skills used to help manage the conflict.

2) *While* volunteers are creating the scenario to be used in the role-play, an observer (using Work Sheet **4-M**) watches their interaction and the dynamic that takes place during this process.

All the case studies are to be used as a means of having fun while improving communication skills.

CONCLUSION

Whenever two or more people are involved in a relationship or in a work situation, conflicts will occur. Setting goals, choosing methods of implementing programs, working out different value systems or factual information not being communicated clearly can be causes for conflicts to arise. Nobody likes conflict. But with detachment, humility and a good sense of humor, it will not be fatal. The important thing is to see conflicts as opportunities for growth. The following work sheets help people learn to communicate in a healthy way and then move beyond immediate setbacks and crises. Take the risk to manage conflicts among friends and co-workers. The reward is greater depth of insight and joy in interacting with others. Options, alternatives, creativity and "grace" flourish only in a free and open atmosphere. It takes vigilance and courage to create and maintain that kind of organization.

ADDITIONAL RESOURCES

Covey, Stephen R., *The 7 Habits of Highly Effective People*. New York: Simon & Schuster. 1990.

Kelly, Maureen, M.A., *The Dysfunctional Parish Staff: Transforming Conflict Into Compassionate Ministry*. Cincinnati, OH: St. Anthony Press. 1992.

Morrison, Emily Kittle, *Working With Volunteers, Skills for Leadership*. Tucson, AZ: Fisher Books. 1988. Chap. 12.

Sweetser, Thomas, S.J. & Carol Holden, *Leadership in a Successful Parish*. Kansas City, MO: Sheed & Ward. 1987, 1992. Pp. 95-108.

4-A

HOW DO YOU USUALLY HANDLE CONFLICTS?

After each of the following techniques indicate whether you use it **frequently, occasionally** or **rarely**. Upon completion, the **key** at the bottom of the page can help identify the style of conflict management being used most frequently.

		Frequently	Occasionally	Rarely
1.	Avoid the person/situation	_____	_____	_____
2.	Change the subject	_____	_____	_____
3.	Try to understand the other person's view	_____	_____	_____
4.	Turn the conflict into a joke	_____	_____	_____
5.	Admit that you are wrong even if you do not believe you are	_____	_____	_____
6.	Give in	_____	_____	_____
7.	Apologize	_____	_____	_____
8.	Identify what you agree on and disagree on to focus the issue	_____	_____	_____
9.	Reach a compromise	_____	_____	_____
10.	Pretend to agree	_____	_____	_____
11.	Get another person to decide who is right	_____	_____	_____
12.	Threaten the other person	_____	_____	_____
13.	Fight it out physically	_____	_____	_____
14.	Whine or complain until you get your way	_____	_____	_____
15.	Play the martyr: give in	_____	_____	_____
16.	Don't show up for meetings	_____	_____	_____
17.	Give a little, get a little of your way	_____	_____	_____

KEY:
FLIGHT: 1,2,4,16. ACCOMMODATION: 5,6,7,10,15.
COMPROMISE: 3,8,9,17. WIN/LOSE: 11,12,13,14.

LOOKING AT THE CONFLICT

4-B

The following questions can help you reflect on a conflict situation you are, or were involved in, and provide a perspective that may help you manage the experience. After completing these questions, reflect on your comments and share them with another person. Listen for new insights regarding your situation. In doing this exercise you may come to a better understanding and sense of direction for resolving the conflict.

Recall a conflict situation that you were involved in within the past three months:

Who was involved? _____

Describe the situation: _____
_____
_____
_____

Was the conflict over facts, goals, methods, or values? How did this affect the intensity of the conflict? Explain.
_____
_____
_____
_____
_____

How was the conflict managed? **(Avoidance, Accommodation, Compromise, Win/Lose Win/Win.)** Explain:
_____
_____
_____
_____
_____

If you did not use a **Win/Win** solution but you feel it is appropriate to do so, what skills would be best to use? (Creative/Active Listening, The "I-Statement," or SANE approach.) Explain:
_____
_____
_____
_____

WORK SHEET ON CONFLICT MANAGEMENT

4-C

The Turning Point For Groups

Conflict is sometimes caused by forces outside of our control. Examples: time commitments, deadlines, illness, etc. List the **sources** of conflict and **resources** available for managing conflict. These could come from within the group as well as from outside the group. Share these responses, first with one other group member, then as a total group. List the **sources** and **resources** on newsprint.

SOURCES OF CONFLICT

From Inside The Group	From Outside The Group

RESOURCES AVAILABLE FOR MANAGING CONFLICT

From Inside The Group	From Outside The Group

Following your discussion, what commitments are you willing to make personally and as a group? Take time to fill in this section quietly then share it with your group.

COMMITMENTS FOR FUTURE INTERACTION

Personal Commitments	Commitments from the Group

APPROPRIATE STYLE OF CONFLICT MANAGEMENT

4-D

Describe several conflicts you are experiencing and identify which method of conflict management is most appropriate in each situation: Avoidance, Accommodation, Compromise, Win/Lose, or Win/Win.

Conflict:_____
_____
_____

Method:_____
Reason:_____
_____
_____
_____

Conflict:_____
_____
_____

Method:_____
Reason:_____
_____
_____
_____

Conflict:_____
_____
_____

Method:_____
Reason:_____
_____
_____
_____

PRACTICING HOW TO MANAGE CONFLICT
CASE STUDY ONE

This exercise is to be used as a role-play (with **4-E2**) allowing two participants to practice the *WIN/WIN* method of conflict management. The participants read their part quietly before beginning the dialogue. The exercise can also be used in conjunction with the **Observer Work Sheet 4-H**. The observer's role is to give feedback to the individuals regarding the skills used in the conversation or the need to adjust their dialogue moving more toward use of the Win/Win skills.

PASTORAL CARE STAFF MEMBER
(Use with Music Director Role)

- You are the part-time pastoral care person on staff.

- Your role is to visit the homebound and elderly.

- You also do counseling for people needing both pastoral support and physical assistance.

- You have fixed up your office for counseling.

- You have reserved Fridays for counseling appointments because the only other day at work is for communion calls and visiting the homebound.

- Unfortunately, your office is next to the music director's office.

- On Fridays the music director is usually practicing music for the weekend liturgies on an electric piano.

- It's very distracting to your counseling.

- You have tried to talk to the music director about this but there has not been much improvement.

- You are getting very upset about this and are thinking about going to the pastor to complain, or even just going over and pulling the plug on that #$%^& ({} electric piano.

4-E2

PRACTICING HOW TO MANAGE CONFLICT
CASE STUDY ONE

This exercise is to be used as a role-play (with **4-E1**) allowing two participants to practice the *WIN/WIN* method of conflict management. The participants read their part quietly before beginning the dialogue. The exercise can also be used in conjunction with the **Observer Work Sheet 4-H**. The observer's role is to give feedback to the individuals regarding the skills used in the conversation or the need to adjust their dialogue moving more toward use of the Win/Win skills.

MUSIC DIRECTOR
(Use with Director of Religious Education Role)

- You are the music director of the parish.

- Your role is to provide quality music for liturgy in the parish and school.

- You are cramped for space. The choir practice space is also used for a classroom during the week.

- As a result, you have to do your preparation and practice of music in your office.

- That's frustrating enough, but the pastoral care person in the office next door complains about your electric piano. Says it's too loud.

- You've toned down as much as you can, but you do have to hear what the drums and instruments will sound like, which you can simulate on the piano.

- The only time you have to practice for the weekend liturgies is on Fridays because you teach music in the school the other days.

4-F1

PRACTICING HOW TO MANAGE CONFLICT
CASE STUDY TWO

This exercise is to be used as a role-play (with **4-F2**) allowing two participants to practice the *WIN/WIN* method of conflict management. The participants read their part quietly before beginning the dialogue. The exercise can also be used in conjunction with the **Observer Work Sheet 4-H**. The observer's role is to give feedback to the individuals regarding the skills used in the conversation or the need to adjust their dialogue moving more toward use of the Win/Win skills.

ASSOCIATE PASTOR
(Use with Director of Religious Education Role)

- You are the Associate of the parish.

- Your day off is Tuesday.

- The staff is planning a day away for reflection/sharing.

- You said that you would be willing to give up your day off if no other time could be found.

- You were away on vacation (much deserved) last week when the staff settled on a date.

- They picked February 14th.

- This so happens to be the once-in-a-year outing and celebration for the priests who are part of a football pool each year. The money that is left over from the year's wagers is used for a fun day.

- You asked if another day could be found for the staff day away and you received a short but definite answer "no" from the person making arrangements.

- You are not going to miss the annual outing with your friends!

4-F2

PRACTICING HOW TO MANAGE CONFLICT
CASE STUDY TWO

This exercise is to be used as a role-play (with **4-F1**) allowing two participants to practice the *WIN/WIN* method of conflict management. The participants read their part quietly before beginning the dialogue. The exercise can also be used in conjunction with the **Observer Work Sheet 4-H**. The observer's role is to give feedback to the individuals regarding the skills used in the conversation or the need to adjust their dialogue moving more toward use of the Win/Win skills.

DIRECTOR OF RELIGIOUS EDUCATION
(Use with Associate Pastor Role)

- You are the director of religious education.

- You are already overworked.

- But you did agree to arrange a staff day away.

- After much negotiation and scheduling you have found a date that all can accept, Valentine's Day!

- At the last staff meeting everyone agreed to be there and they even worked on an agenda that everyone thought would be not only helpful to the staff, but fun.

- Since that meeting, you have run into a snag.

- The associate pastor was not at the last staff meeting but he said before leaving on vacation that he would abide by whatever the staff agreed to, even giving up his day off.

- Now he comes to tell you that the one date chosen he can't make. He has a prior commitment he can't break.

- Your response to him was not very civil.

- You let him know that you were not willing to go back and find another date, take it or leave it!

4-G1

PRACTICING HOW TO MANAGE CONFLICT

CASE STUDY THREE

This exercise is to be used as a role-play (with **4-G2**) allowing two participants to practice the *WIN/WIN* method of conflict management. The participants read their part quietly before beginning the dialogue. The exercise can also be used in conjunction with the **Observer Work Sheet 4-H**. The observer's role is to give feedback to the individuals regarding the skills used in the conversation or the need to adjust their dialogue moving more toward use of the Win/Win skills.

PASTOR
(Use with Youth Director)

- You are the pastor of the parish.

- The youth director is having difficulties getting teenagers involved in the youth program.

- Parents of the youth are not happy with what the youth director is doing: too many dances and movies. The same group of kids come.

- The youth director is off doing his own thing and often misses staff meetings.

- You decide to meet with the youth director and tell him his contract will not be renewed for the following year.

- The youth director is just now at your door.

4-G2

PRACTICING HOW TO MANAGE CONFLICT

CASE STUDY THREE

This exercise is to be used as a role-play (with **4-G1**) allowing two participants to practice using the *WIN/WIN* method of conflict management. The participants read their part quietly before beginning the dialogue. The exercise can also be used in conjunction with the **Observer Work Sheet 4-H**. The observer's role is to give feedback to the individuals regarding the skills used in the conversation or the need to adjust their dialogue moving more toward use of the Win/Win skills.

YOUTH DIRECTOR
(Use with Pastor)

- This is your first year as a parish youth director.

- You feel you are doing a good job.

- You started out slowly and have been building a core group of teen leaders.

- You used the attraction principle by sponsoring many socializing events, dances and movies.

- It has been so time consuming that you have had to miss several staff meetings.

- You're glad the pastor asked you in for this chat.

- Being happy with your work, you have decided to ask the pastor for a raise next year. This seems to be a good time.

- You are just now walking into the pastor's office.

OBSERVER WORK SHEET (A)

4-H

Your task is to observe the interaction of the two people doing the role-play. Take note of the skills being used or avoided. Share your observations regarding their use of the conflict management skills. This will help them identify when they have a good grasp of the skills and where they need more practice.

Identify the skills being used:_____
_____
_____
_____
_____
_____
_____
_____
_____
_____

Identify places where the skills were **NOT USED** and give suggestions for a more favorable outcome:
_____
_____
_____
_____
_____
_____
_____
_____
_____
_____
_____

GROUP CASE STUDY
CONFLICT SITUATION ONE

Instructions: Role-play this scene in one of two ways: 1) The worst possible way disregarding any conflict management skills you may know or 2) the best possible way using the appropriate skills. Following the role-play invite the observers (audience) to discuss the group dynamics (not the content), pointing out the areas where appropriate skills were used. Also, identify the areas where the lack of appropriate skills was quite evident. Give suggestions as to what skills would have been appropriate.

Getting Started: Use six volunteers to set the scene for the role-play. One person reads the situation out loud. Be sure everyone understands what it is about. Figure out who will play what character. Arrange whatever props are available. Outline the dialogue to be used in the role-play but don't prepare too well. Let it unfold before the audience. Good luck.

Focus: The Liturgy Committee plans a communal penance service and presents it to the staff. Everyone likes the plan except the associate pastor.

Characters: Religious Ed./Liturgy Coordinator   Youth Director
Pastor   Principal
Associate Pastor   Pastoral Minister/Parish Visitor

Time Limits: Preparation 20 minutes
Presentation 10 minutes

Situation: The Liturgy Committee is to plan the Penance Service for the upcoming parish mission. A special meeting to plan this event is called and all of the staff are invited. A special attempt is made to get the priests to come, however, their schedules prevent them from attending. The Religious Education/Liturgy Coordinator is the only staff member present at the meeting.

The committee is excited with what they have come up with: a dramatic reading of the woman taken in adultery. Included will be a little role-play with the people writing down a sin. These will be collected and burned as a symbol of God's mercy. Not wanting to leave the priests out of the planning, the committee has purposely left vague the part of the service which involves the individual telling of sins and the way absolution is to be done.

The Religious Education/Liturgy Coordinator presents the plan at the next staff meeting. At first the staff appears interested but then some confusion arises. The pastor and associate are not too sure about some of the *theatrics* in the service. When it gets to the point of deciding where the priests should stand for the confessing of sins and how absolution will be done, the *discussion* begins to break down. The pastor, who is to lead the service, is confused about his role. The associate, who does not like the plan, announces he is not sure he is free that evening. The Religious Education/Liturgy Coordinator is angry because all their work is going down the drain. This would not have happened if the priests had come to the planning meeting. The other three staff members are trying to preserve some level of calm and peace.

After an hour of *discussion,* a modified plan for the communal service is settled upon. The dramatic reading will take place but without the role-play. A symbolic burning of sins will take place but without writing down and collecting the sins. The two priests will be there standing at either side of the communion rail and absolution will be given by the priests together. The rest of the agenda for the staff meeting is postponed until the next meeting since time has run out and everyone is too upset to continue. No one is really satisfied with the outcome but at least the penance service will take place as scheduled. The Religious Education/Liturgy Coordinator and pastor now have the task of telling the Liturgy Committee the outcome. The others leave confused and frustrated.

GROUP CASE STUDY
CONFLICT SITUATION TWO

Instructions: Role-play this scene in one of two ways: 1) The worst possible way disregarding any conflict management skills you may know or 2) the best possible way using the appropriate skills. Following the role-play invite the observers (audience) to discuss the group dynamics (not the content), pointing out the areas where appropriate skills were used. Also, identify the areas where the lack of appropriate skills was quite evident. Give suggestions as to what skills would have been appropriate.

Getting Started: Use six volunteers to set the scene for the role-play. One person reads the situation out loud. Be sure everyone understands what it is about. Figure out who will play what character. Arrange whatever props are available. Outline the dialogue to be used in the role-play but don't prepare too well. Let it unfold before the audience. Good luck.

Focus: The Adult Religious Education Coordinator is asking for help in putting together the Lenten Adult Education program.

Characters:
Adult Religious Ed. Coordinator   Religious Ed. Coordinator
Pastor   Principal
Pastoral Associate   Pastoral Minister/Parish Visitor

Time Limits: Preparation 20 minutes
Presentation 10 minutes

Situation: The parish staff has come together to decide about the Lenten Adult Education program. Some of the staff members have had to give up their day off to attend this special meeting. The Adult DRE starts the meeting thanking everyone profusely for coming and says she needs everyone's ideas for the program. Just when people are getting warmed up and good ideas generated, she announces she has to leave early for a special workshop sponsored by the Religious Education Center. The rest of the staff is surprised and frustrated by her leaving. Protesting as she goes out the door, she tells them to keep thinking of good ideas. The staff, realizing it is worthless to continue without her, dissolve the meeting with small talk and coffee.

The following week, the Adult Coordinator arranges a second meeting with the staff on the same issue. Arriving happily and apologizing for calling another meeting, adds this shouldn't take much time since most of the Lenten program is already set. She has put it together the night before and now wants to check it out with everyone on staff.

The program is presented and feedback is asked for. The staff likes the presentation and approves it except for one area which they object to. The discussion goes on for half an hour at which point the Coordinator announces she has a counseling session and the person is already waiting for her. As she leaves, she thanks everyone for their input and says the program will be adjusted as a result of the staff's feedback. The pastor tries to get her to clarify the meaning of *adjusting the program*. She remarks that all will be fine and rushes out of the room. The rest of the staff throw up their arms in despair. They admit it is a good program but feel uneasy about that one area of discussion. They feel their suggestions were not taken seriously and they don't have much involvement in the program. Realizing not much more can be done, they leave to continue their own tasks.

GROUP CASE STUDY
CONFLICT SITUATION THREE

Instructions: Role-play this scene in one of two ways: 1) The worst possible way disregarding any conflict management skills you may know or 2) the best possible way using the appropriate skills. Following the role-play invite the observers (audience) to discuss the group dynamics (not the content), pointing out the areas where appropriate skills were used. Also, identify the areas where the lack of appropriate skills was quite evident. Give suggestions as to what skills would have been appropriate.

Getting Started: Use six volunteers to set the scene for the role-play. One person reads the situation out loud. Be sure everyone understands what it is about. Figure out who will play what character. Arrange whatever props are available. Outline the dialogue to be used in the role-play but don't prepare too well. Let it unfold before the audience. Good luck.

Focus: The Pastoral Minister has been asked to arrange a date for the parish team to get away for a team day together.

Characters: Pastoral Minister / Parish Visitor   Pastoral Associate
Pastor   Business Manager
Adult/Youth Director   Religious Ed. Coordinator

Time Limits: Preparation 20 minutes
Presentation 10 minutes

Situation: You comprise a parish team of six that has been in operation for two years. For the most part you have been successful. You care for each other but find that parish ministry leaves little time for team interaction. The group decided to take a day off next month for a team retreat. The Pastoral Minister volunteered to contact a retreat center not far from the parish to find available dates. This is done immediately and each team member is contacted to see what would be the best available date. It is soon apparent that it will be impossible for everyone to agree on a date. Although receiving much affirmation from everyone, a suitable date is not found.

At the next team meeting, it is suggested that the retreat be put off for two months so a suitable date for all can be found. "By all means, no difficulty, do it, keep at it, you are doing a great job," are the responses.

Calling back the retreat house, another list of dates is chosen and once again each team member is contacted. Once again, a suitable date for all cannot be found. Everyone is too busy and personal schedules always get in the way. Her frustration is apparent since even though everyone has said the retreat day was a high priority no one is willing to let go of other commitments so a date can be found. These commitments include the pastor's day off, the Business Manager's swimming schedule, the DRE's support group and the Pastoral Associate's community night. The retreat house is called to cancel the dates they had been holding for the parish team.

At the next meeting a report is given of her efforts and the announcement that the team retreat will have to wait until later. Inside she finds it difficult because her heart was set on having this time away from the parish with the team. She lets it go and they go on to the next item of business on the agenda.

4-L

GROUP CASE STUDY
CONFLICT SITUATION FOUR

Instructions: Role-play this scene in one of two ways: 1) The worst possible way disregarding any conflict management skills you may know or 2) the best possible way using the appropriate skills. Following the role-play invite the observers (audience) to discuss the group dynamics (not the content), pointing out the areas where appropriate skills were used. Also, identify the areas where the lack of appropriate skills was quite evident. Give suggestions as to what skills would have been appropriate.

Getting Started: Use six volunteers to set the scene for the role-play. One person reads the situation out loud. Be sure everyone understands what it is about. Figure out who will play what character. Arrange whatever props are available. Outline the dialogue to be used in the role-play but don't prepare too well. Let it unfold before the audience. Good luck.

Focus: A relationship between the associate pastor and the principal is creating a stir. People are wondering what's going on.

Characters:
- Pastor
- Associate Pastor
- Adult/Youth Director
- Religious Ed. Coordinator
- Principal
- Pastoral Minister/Parish Visitor

Time Limits:
Preparation 20 minutes
Presentation 10 minutes

Situation: The other staff members have been noticing that the associate and principal are spending quite a bit of time together. True, they are both working in the same area, putting together a good religious education curriculum, for the school. They are also hearing reports from teachers and parents about how they both carry on, lots of kidding, laughing, hardly professional.

A teacher complained to the pastor that the associate was neglecting his 8th grade religion class by being in the principal's office instead. The associate contends the class was doing a library assignment with individual study and research as part of the program he and the principal had set up.

The pastor's response was to let it pass since the associate was doing so well in other areas. The pastor also knew that if he lost this associate another one would not be assigned to the parish. Now other members of the staff are approaching the pastor wondering what is going on between the associate and principal. Is it getting out of hand? The pastor's comment is that he trusts them both and changed the subject.

The next staff meeting, the principal and associate make a joint report about the new religious education program. Some of the staff members bring up the subject of image. The pastor, giving non-verbal signs, decides it would be better to let this matter pass. The principal and associate, aware of what is happening, are relieved that nothing was said. The rest of the staff are concerned but did not know how to bring up this subject in a way that the two of them will listen. As a result, the moment slipped by and the next item on the agenda taken up.

After the meeting, the pastor mentions to the Adult Education Coordinator and the Religious Ed. Coordinator that he too is concerned but since they are adults, he is sure they can take care of themselves. Nothing more is said on the matter.

OBSERVER'S WORK SHEET (B)

Your task is to observe the interaction of the people in the group and watch how they deal with each other as they are creating the role-play. Do not critique the task they are working on. Rather, watch for how well they deal with one another as they work on their task. In particular, watch for these aspects to see if they occur and how they are handled by group members. [Use with Work Sheets 4-I - 4-L.]

1. Do you notice any conflicts, disagreements or misunderstandings between group members? If so, briefly describe what they are.
   _____
   _____
   _____
   _____

2. If any misunderstandings or conflicts have occurred, did anyone in the group try to help out and seek to clarify the situation? Describe how this happened.
   _____
   _____
   _____
   _____

3. Do you notice any one person taking over and dominating the group so as to accomplish the task that is to be done? If so, describe how this happened.
   _____
   _____
   _____
   _____

4. Do you notice any person(s) who appears to be left out of the task and discussion, or who appears to be opting out of the interaction. Describe how the group deals with this.
   _____
   _____
   _____
   _____

5. Are there any other significant observations you would like to make about the way the group members are interacting? If yes, please mention these here.
   _____
   _____
   _____
   _____

4-M

5 | STRESS MANAGEMENT

INTRODUCTION A selection process for Pastoral Council members took place three months ago. At first the chairperson was encouraged by the contagious enthusiasm of the four new members. After last night's meeting, things began to change.

One new member suggested that the council do some long-range parish planning since St. Mary's has doubled its size in the last three years. Younger families are moving into the area and the school is filled to capacity. The person also noted that families who have lived in the parish since its founding, 25 years ago, are experiencing feelings of alienation. Their needs are not being met. It seems to them that more attention is being given to the newcomers. With an increase of membership and all this demands, the three staff members are showing signs of burnout. The Director of Religious Education is even considering resigning. With this in mind, the new member suggested that it may be a good opportunity to hire an outside facilitator experienced in doing parish planning.

Another new council member, has been a parishioner since the beginning of the parish. He sees himself as a representative of the founders of the parish community, "the old-timers," who built this place from scratch. They feel that full authority should be given back to the pastor. The present council has too much power and influence in running the parish. They are even suggesting that the homeless make use of the parish hall as an overnight shelter facility this winter!

The two new members are raising concerns that could suggest some *long and intense discussions* at the council meetings. It implies the formation of new committees to encourage more leadership from the parishioners. It also means convening parish town hall meetings to keep the communication open between the leadership and people.

Taking a deep breath, the chairperson begins to imagine the time commitments for the next several months. "How will I be able to balance all of this activity with my personal life commitments? My daughter is getting married in two months. I have out-of-town relatives coming in one week before the wedding. Not to mention that my boss left me in charge of the office for the next two weeks while she is out of town on business."

If this scenario, or something like it, sounds familiar, it's time to sound the *ALARM*!

WHAT IS STRESS?

Stress is a normal part of life. We **need** it! It's the spice of life adding surprise, challenge and excitement. **Stress** is a "non-specific response of the body to a demand or change." Starting a new job, having a baby, buying a home, graduating from college, or bowling a perfect 300 game can be occasions of stress. These moments are accompanied by feelings of joy, elation, relief and a sense of accomplishment. However, getting a divorce, failing a test, losing a job, or getting a parking ticket, can also be occasions of stress. They are accompanied by feelings of anger, frustration and disappointment. Our body cannot tell the difference between positive and negative stress. In either case, our body experiences the same effects: a quick surge of adrenaline, an increase in heartbeat or blood pressure, a rise in blood sugar. Stress is like body temperature: if it's too low or too high, a person cannot survive, but the right balance keeps the mind and body strong.

FORMULA FOR STRESS

> Stress = stressors + stress response

*Stress is the experience of a change or demand placed on us. The change, or demand itself, is called the **stressor**. The way we choose to respond to the situation is the **stress response**.* It's important to use stress in a positive way so it doesn't become *distress or bad stress*.

A heated discussion at a council meeting can be a *stressor*. The chairperson becomes aware of the stress as body muscles tense and a headache persists. The way one chooses to respond to the discussion is the *stress response*. Here are some options. The chairperson could: 1) walk out of the room and not return, 2) shout over the group to stop the discussion, leaving it unfinished, 3) call for silence so everyone can think quietly for two minutes, then resume the conversation in a calmer atmosphere, or 4) ask the group to address the pros and cons of the issue so more information can be acquired.

Choosing an option such as #1 or #2 may suggest that the stress experienced by the chairperson is unhealthy. Methods of dealing with it seem counterproductive. On the other hand, choosing #3 or #4 suggests a healthy stress response. The chairperson may experience this stressful situation as a means of focusing everyone's energy. Encouraging the group to be creative in identifying possible options may be the best solution. In this way, the group can experience a healthy and life-giving situation. It all depends on a person's stress resistance. How well has he/she developed a positive mental attitude?

Some people love challenges. They experience a stressful situation as an excellent way to achieve a goal. Their creative juices start flowing and unleashed energy begins to work. People with this type of personality react to stressful situations with a zest for life, a sense of purpose, an avenue for growth.

Other people experience stressful situations as moments of powerlessness. They feel threatened and alienated. Becoming overwhelmed with the disruptions they feel there is no way out. If an individual has not developed good support systems or health practices, stressful life events can produce more strain and eventually cause them illness. The diagram below illustrates how these areas are related.

With a strong mind, body, and spirit an individual is better able to cope with stressful situations. Work Sheet **5-A** can help identify a person's current level of stress resistance.

Stress affects us as a whole person. We experience symptoms of stress exhaustion not only in our bodies, but also in our emotional reactions, our mental state, our relationships with others and our spiritual life. Being aware of this may help a person identify early signs of stress exhaustion, preventing depression and other serious results of stress. Work Sheet **5-B**, Stress Exhaustion Symptoms, provides a checklist of these signs.

BUILDING UP STRESS RESISTANCE

Taking control of one's life and developing a healthy positive mental attitude transforms stressful events into moments of growth. Here are a few important reminders.

- Develop a support system of friends with whom you can share ideas and talk freely. These are people with whom you can be yourself, yet who will challenge you to develop and use your gifts and talents.
- Take time to exercise and eat healthy foods. Keeping your body in good shape inside and out is important.

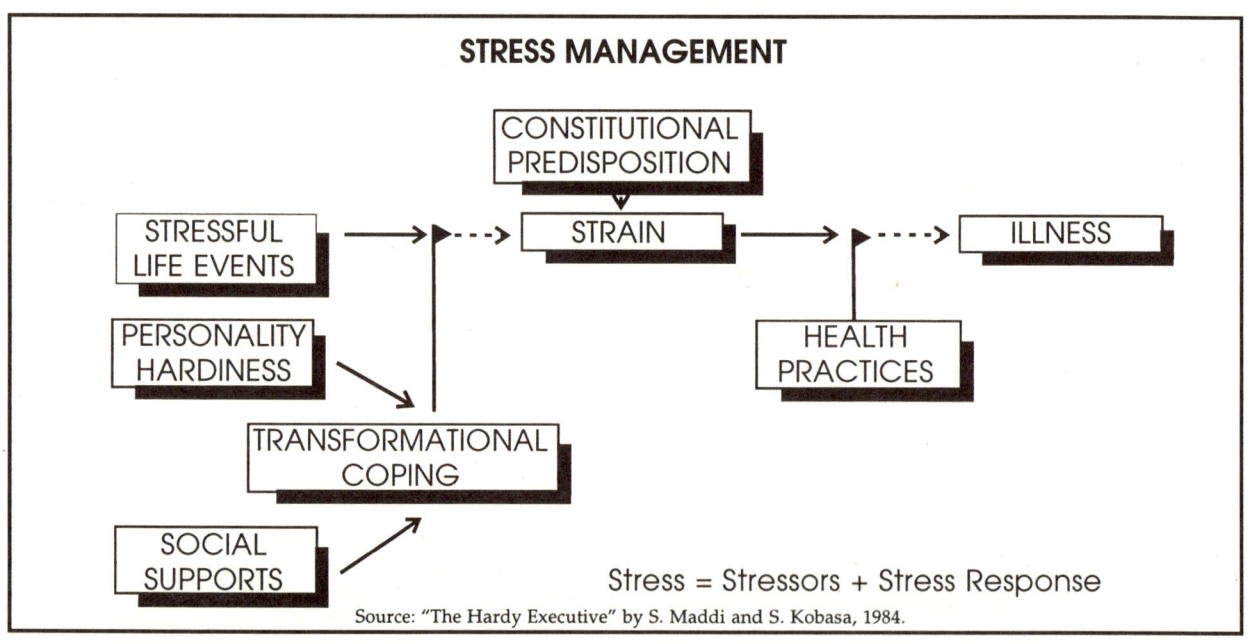

STRESS MANAGEMENT

Stress = Stressors + Stress Response

Source: "The Hardy Executive" by S. Maddi and S. Kobasa, 1984.

- Spend quiet time away from distraction and noise. Get in touch with your spiritual center.
- Look at alternative ways of dealing with the stressors. First name the *stressor*. Then, be creative in seeking options for the healthy *stress response*.

Work Sheet **5-C** suggests specific ways of using the **AAAbc's** of stress management. First identify the source of stress. Then uncover ways to **A**LTER it, **A**VOID it, or **A**CCEPT it by . . . **b**uilding resistance, or **c**hanging your perception. All these approaches can be effective techniques for coping with stress. Making the proper choice, however, in a given situation is not easy. Choose the method that is best for *you*.

Work Sheet **5-D** provides a framework to identify a stressful situation, explore alternatives for a stress response, and then choose the best approach. Work Sheets **5-E** through **5-I** provide scenarios for practicing the AAAbc's of stress. Be creative! Uncover various options and discuss them with other people before choosing the best approach. These exercises can provide positive ways of dealing with stressful situations, instead of feeling defeated by them.

WHAT IS BURNOUT?

Burnout is a response to chronic, everyday stress rather than an occasional crisis. It often appears among individuals who do "people oriented work" of some kind.

People involved in ministry are prime candidates for burnout and need to take precautions by finding a healthy balance of work and relaxation. Their role as minister is never ending. Someone will always be in need of their services. The type of ministry performed does not always have visible results. Because of this, it is difficult to experience a sense of achievement. Much of a minister's work helps people internally or spiritually and goes unnoticed. Ministers are expected to be available and pleasant to everyone. They often put their own needs and feelings aside even when they are completely drained.

When people become too emotionally involved and feel overwhelmed by the demands placed on them by others, they begin to feel emotionally exhausted. This can lead to viewing people as inanimate objects, making it easier to disregard them and their needs. A negative attitude toward others grows to such an extent that the victim of burnout begins to feel inadequate. Feelings of self-esteem are diminished.

Can burnout be prevented? YES, by all means! Let's identify the stages of burnout and the antidotes that can provide assistance to individuals as the stages progress. By making use of these aids a person can abort the burnout process, enabling the individual to regain a healthy mind, body and soul.

STAGES OF BURNOUT

STAGE I: Enthusiasm

People who are filled with endless energy commit themselves wholeheartedly to projects without setting any limits. They are usually perfectionists and great achievers. Their enthusiasm is so contagious that others are energized by their presence. No task seems too big for them to accomplish, especially if the project is people-oriented. These individuals are good candidates for burnout. They are often found in the helping professions.

Antidote

Individuals need to know that the ideal they are striving to achieve is quite different from the reality of the situation. The ideal and the real may never meet. Having a good idea of what can reasonably be accomplished is helpful. Allow for innovation and creativity but stay within realistic limits of time and energy. A clear job description can help focus priorities and commitments.

STAGE II: Stagnation

When an individual begins experiencing signs of exhaustion they may be entering the phase of stagnation. A person starts feeling stuck in a rut. Everything is seen as routine. There is a loss of energy. A person starts questioning his/her ability to function and the purpose of his/her role. It becomes harder to make simple decisions and some of their judgments are not very good.

Antidote

It is advisable to find support persons to challenge you. Explore reasons for doing specific tasks. Try accomplishing things in new ways. Change the environment, even if it means moving furniture, relocating to another place, or redecorating an office. Rearrange your schedule or change your mode of operating.

STAGE III: Frustration

When a person cannot handle the routine and they have no creativity left, they begin feeling frustrated and defeated. Feelings of anger become intense and they show signs of withdrawal by becoming less involved with work, family and friends. They experience a decrease in appetite, sleep, sex, and health. For these individuals, there is no longer a distinction between work and free time.

Antidote

Obtaining professional help and advice at this stage is imperative. Look at three important areas of your life: physical, emotional and spiritual. From the physical perspective, try to increase exercise activities to relieve some of the stress. Eat well-balanced meals and get enough rest. Take time for relaxation and leisure.

Emotionally, try to put some meaning into your life. A special friend may be an important key to this element. Take time to get away and relax. Put things into perspective. Keeping a journal is a way of listening to some inner wisdom. Share these thoughts with your friends and ask for feedback.

Look at the spiritual component that can be the center of your wellness. Find someone to be a spiritual director or mentor for you. Risk openness and reflect on the values of your life. Dialogue with your pain and feelings. Listen from within and reflect with others to discern the meaning. Try to understand the values of a job and its relationship to a personal life.

STAGE IV: Apathy

When individuals reach this stage of burnout, they have given up. They withdraw from the life around them with a feeling of "who cares?" Their attitude is negative and cynical. Friends are viewed as enemies. Joy has no place in their lives. Depression sets in and a chemical dependency is a danger, offering the illusion that this will make things better.

Antidote

There is not too much left for individuals to do except to make an extreme change in life. One option is that they can take a leave of absence from their job. Another option is to change jobs completely. Finding something new to do in a totally different environment would be best. These changes may allow for the birth of some new creativity.

The hope is that individuals will be cautious and not wait until the last phase of burnout to seek help. One factor in preventing burnout is the awareness of a person's reaction to situations in the work place. Consistent irritability may be a signal that things are going awry. Observing events and recording one's reaction to them provides information for discovering patterns that could lead to burnout. Reflection questions on Work Sheet **5-J** are helpful in "taking your pulse." Keep a good support system in place while doing ministry. Listen to your body's symptoms of pain, tiredness and cynicism. They may be saying something very important to you. Pay attention and attend to your needs as soon as possible! Ministers also need ministering!

CONCLUSION

One image that comes to mind is a juggler throwing several balls up in the air. The skill in keeping some balls in the air while holding others in the hand, ever so briefly, calls for concentration. The objects played with can be anything from feather-weight scarves, soft balls, or even flaming sticks. Once the routine is learned the juggler can add excitement and intrigue to the show. Between performances, it is important that the juggler rest the mind and body to stay alert and agile.

Our council chairperson, at the beginning of this chapter, reminds us that this juggling act takes place in our everyday life. The time and energy that is spent juggling the various commitments to family, to work, and to parish are not easy. Sometimes we juggle the feather-weight scarves. These are symbols of the fun-filled stresses in life. Other times, we are struggling to juggle the flaming sticks, symbols of the difficult challenges that are expressions of life's distress. It takes practice to keep a good balance and have a positive mental attitude toward all these experiences.

With the help of these resources, stress becomes the spice of life, challenging you to be creative with your stress response. Pay attention to signals from within. Be grateful for friends who love you enough to say, "STOP! Take care of yourself!" They are the key to helping you stay happy and healthy.

ADDITIONAL RESOURCES

Maslach, Christina, *Burnout – The Cost of Caring*. New Jersey: Prentice Hill, Englewood Cliffs. 1982.

Pines, Ayala and Elliot Aronson, *Career Burnout, Causes & Cures*. New York: The Free Press, Macmillan, Inc. 1988.

Potter, Dr. Beverly, *Beating Job Burnout, How to Transform Work Pressure into Productivity*. Berkeley, CA: Harbor Publishing Inc. 1993.

Sanford, John A., *Ministry Burnout*. New York: Paulist Press. 1982.

Tubesing, Nancy Loving, EdD and Donald A. Tubesing, MDiv, Phd, *Structured Exercises in Stress Management*, A Whole Person Handbook, Duluth, MN: Whole Person Press. 1983.

Welch, I. David, Donald C. Medeiros, George A. Tate, *Beyond Burnout, How to Enjoy Your Job Again When You've Just About Had Enough*. New Jersey: Prentice Hall, Inc. 1982.

HOW STRESS-RESISTANT ARE YOU?

Rate each item from 1 (almost always) to 5 (never) according to how the statement pertains to you. Answer every item, even if it does not apply to you (for instance, if you don't smoke, give yourself 1, not 0).

1. I eat at least one hot balanced meal a day. _____
2. I get 7 to 8 hours of sleep at least four nights a week. _____
3. I give and receive affection regularly. _____
4. I have at least one relative within 50 miles on whom I can rely. _____
5. I exercise to the point of perspiration at least two times weekly. _____
6. I limit myself to less than half a pack of cigarettes. _____
7. I consume fewer than 5 alcoholic drinks a week. _____
8. I am an appropriate weight for my body build. _____
9. My income covers my basic expenses. _____
10. I get strength from my religious beliefs. _____
11. I regularly attend social activities. _____
12. I have a network of close friends and acquaintances. _____
13. I have one or more friends to confide in about personal matters. _____
14. I am in good health including eyesight, hearing, teeth. _____
15. I am able to speak openly about my feelings: anger, worry, etc. _____
16. I discuss domestic problems: money, chores, etc. with those close to me. _____
17. I have fun at least once a week. _____
18. I can organize my time effectively. _____
19. I drink fewer than three cups of coffee (or other caffeine-rich beverages) a day. _____
20. I take some quiet time during the day. _____

Scoring: Add up your total points
         20-44 You have a hearty resistance to stress.
         45-55 You are somewhat vulnerable to stress.
         56 +   You are very susceptible to stress.

Based on Vulnerability Scale from the Stress Audit by Lyle H. Miller and Alma Dell Smith. Copyright 1983, Biobehavioral Associates, Brookline, Mass. The Walking Magazine, Sept./Oct. 1990.

STRESS EXHAUSTION SYMPTOMS

A. Check the symptoms of stress exhaustion you've noticed lately in yourself. (You may add others.)

PHYSICAL	EMOTIONAL	SPIRITUAL	MENTAL	RELATIONAL
___ appetite loss	___ anxiety	___ emptiness	___ forgetfulness	___ isolation
___ headaches	___ frustration	___ loss of meaning	___ dull senses	___ intolerance
___ tension	___ the "blues"	___ doubt	___ poor concentration	___ resentment
___ fatigue	___ mood swings	___ unforgiving	___ low productivity	___ loneliness
___ insomnia	___ bad temper	___ martyrdom	___ negative attitude	___ lashing out
___ weight change	___ nightmares	___ looking for magic	___ confusion	___ hiding
___ colds	___ crying spells	___ loss of direction	___ lethargy	___ clamming up
___ muscle aches	___ irritability	___ needing to "prove"	___ whirling mind	___ lowered sex drive
___ digestive upsets	___ "no one cares"	___ self	___ no new ideas	___ nagging
___ pounding heart	___ depression	___ cynicism	___ boredom	___ distrust
___ accident prone	___ nervous laugh	___ apathy	___ spacing out	___ fewer contacts with
___ teeth grinding	___ worrying		___ negative self-talk	___ friends
___ rash	___ easily discouraged			___ lack of intimacy
___ restlessness	___ little joy			___ using people
___ foot-tapping				
___ finger-drumming				
___ increased alcohol,				
___ drugs, tobacco use				

B. Circle the ones that cause you most concern. Which ones are you worried about right now?

C. Reflect for a moment on the patterns you see in these stress symptoms.
1) Are most of your symptoms in one area?
2) Are you more concerned about physical symptoms than spiritual ones?
3) Are any areas symptom free?

D. Choose one symptom and dialogue with it. What is it saying to you?

Reprinted with permission. Adapted from *Structured Exercises in Stress Management, Volume 1*, copyright 1983, 1994. Donald A. Tubesing. Published by Whole Person Assoicates Inc, 210 West Michigan, Duluth, MN 55802-1908, 218-727-0500. p. 17-20.

AAAbc's OF STRESS MANAGEMENT

OPTIONS for STRESS RESPONSE:

1. **A**LTER IT   Remove the sources of stress by:
   - Problem-solving
   - Direct communication
   - Planning
   - Time management

2. **A**VOID IT   Get away or prevent the stress by:
   - Letting go
   - Say no
   - Delegate
   - Withdraw
   - Knowing your limits

3. **A**CCEPT IT   Live with it by:

   building your resistance
   - Physically: Exercise, diet, relaxing, etc.
   - Mentally: Affirmation, time off, clear goals, priorities, etc.
   - Socially: Support system, relationships, clear communication, etc.
   - Spiritually: Prayer, worship, faith commitment, meditation, etc.

   Changing your perception
   - Redefining the situation
   - Changing expectations
   - Creating a positive attitude
   - Realizing you do some things well

Note: Different options work better for different people depending on personalities, situations, environment, etc.

Reprinted with permission. Adapted from *Structured Exercises in Stress Management, Volume 1,* copyright 1983, 1984. Donald A. Tubesing. Published by Whole Person Assoicates Inc, 210 West Michigan, Duluth, MN 55802-1908, 218-727-0500. p. 49-52.

AAAbc's of Stress Management

Identify the source of stress:_____

ALTER: How could you remove the source of stress?

AVOID: How could you get away from or prevent the stress?

ACCEPT: How could you live with the stress?

    build up resistance:

    change self/perception:

BEST OPTION: What option do you think is best?

    Following a group discussion what option is chosen?

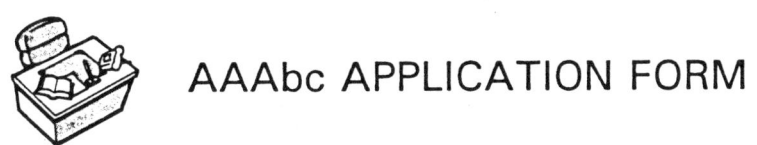

AAAbc APPLICATION FORM

SCENARIO ONE:

There has just been a change of pastors. The new pastor does not seem to like you nor understand what your role is in the church. No matter what you do, he is always critical of your efforts. You are beginning to think you will never be able to please him. What could you do?

Identify source of stress:_____

ALTER: How could you remove the source of stress?

AVOID: How could you get away from or prevent the stress?

ACCEPT: How could you live with the stress?

      build up resistance:

      change self/perception:

BEST OPTION: What option do you think is best?

      Following a group discussion, what option is chosen?

AAAbc APPLICATION FORM

SCENARIO TWO:

You have just moved to the city to take this new job as Director of Religious Education. You don't know anyone in town except for the people at work. The loneliness is starting to get to you, but you are not the kind of person who meets new people easily. You've been spending all your free evenings in your apartment reading or watching TV. You're getting more and more depressed. What could you do?

Identify the source of stress:_____

ALTER: How could you remove the source of stress?

AVOID: How could you get away from or prevent the stress?

ACCEPT: How could you live with the stress?

    build up resistance:

    change self/perception:

BEST OPTION: What option do you think is best?

    Following a group discussion, what option is chosen?

AAAbc APPLICATION FORM

SCENARIO THREE:

You like your job as Pastoral Associate and it pays a reasonable salary but in the current economic climate it's getting harder and harder to make ends meet. Every month is a struggle. You had planned to take a vacation trip this summer but you've decided you'll have to cancel those plans even though your spouse is really counting on going. Now's the time to let your spouse know. What could you do?

Identify the source of stress: _____

ALTER: How could you remove the source of stress?

AVOID: How could you get away from or prevent the stress?

ACCEPT: How could you live with the stress?

    build up resistance:

    change self/perception:

BEST OPTION: What option do you think is best?

    Following a group discussion, what option is chosen?

AAAbc APPLICATION FORM

SCENARIO FOUR:

You have two children in high school. They are basically good kids and helpful around the house, but recently the older one has been neglecting chores and mercilessly bugging the younger one. Tonight it was complaints about dinner, an argument about whose turn it was for dishes and slamming doors when you mentioned homework. You feel wound up and ready to snap if you observe one more act of rebellion. What could you do?

Identify the source of stress:_____

ALTER: How could you remove the source of stress?

AVOID: How could you get away from or prevent the stress?

ACCEPT: How could you live with the stress?

      build up resistance:

      change self/perception:

BEST OPTION: What option do you think is best?

      Following a group discussion, what option is chosen?

AAAbc APPLICATION FORM

SCENARIO FIVE:

This business of being chairperson of the finance committee is getting to you. The committee is trying to put some order into the accounts, demanding purchase orders and budgets and such. The staff members and volunteers are not used to this approach and feel curtailed in their ministry. They use many acts of passive aggression against you, not handing in expense accounts, not reporting repair needs, not turning off lights. It's almost more than you can stand. What could you do?

Identify the source of stress:_____

ALTER: How could you remove the source of stress?

AVOID: How could you get away from or prevent the stress?

ACCEPT: How could you live with the stress?

      build up resistance:

      change self/perception:

BEST OPTION: What option do you think is best?

      Following a group discussion, what option is chosen?

BURNOUT PREVENTION
Taking Your Pulse. . .

1. Name the ministry areas you are most enthusiastic about. . .

2. How much of your time is spent in this area?
   More than enough ____, *enough* ____, *not enough* ____. Explain:

3. What is your level of satisfaction with the results of your work?
   Low ____, *medium* ____, *high* ____. Explain:

4. How is your creativity being challenged in this area of ministry?

5. What changes can be made to bring new life and less routine to the task?

6. Name the people who are supporting or mentoring you in this area of ministry.

6 | PLANNING: MISSION AND PRESENT SITUATION

INTRODUCTION A parish is slated to close. The diocese does not have enough priests to go around. Once the pastor retires, the parish community will be "assumed" by the neighboring parish in the next town twenty miles away.

The people's response was immediate. "You are *not* going to close us down. We are a viable community. We have a right to stay open!"

The diocese, not wanting to alienate the congregation, said that it would hold off its decision for one year. By that time it would need evidence that the parish could survive and that its people were being well-served. "Come up with a plan and we will see what we can do." Planning had not been a tradition in the parish, but the council decided to give it a try.

This scenario is not unusual. Many parishes function with little or no thought about planning until a crisis happens. All resources are then focused on the problem until a solution is found. The planning process then comes to a halt, until the next crisis occurs.

Is this the way to bring life to a parish? It is not by chance that a parish responds to its people's needs, reflects gospel values, models Christian service and provides life-giving worship. These things are the fruit of a carefully coordinated pastoral plan. A parish that is alive has a tradition of planning.

Effective planning is shaped by five questions:

1. Who are we?
2. Where are we now?
3. Where are we going?
4. How do we get there?
5. How close did we come?

Four of these questions follow a progression around a planning cycle.

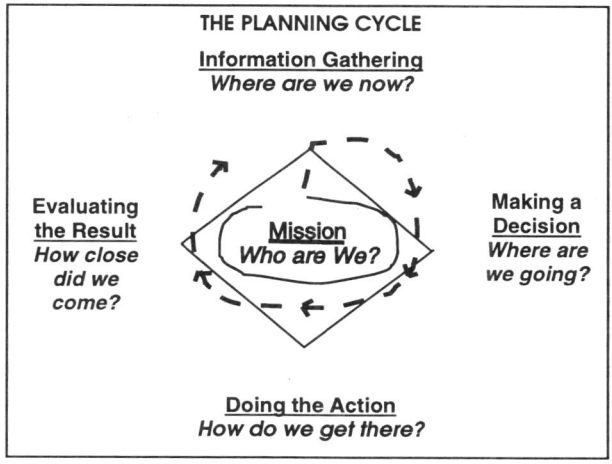

The planning cycle applies in all situations, large or small. Suppose a social committee is planning a summer picnic. They start with the information gathering stage by answering the question, *Where Are We Now?* They investigate when and where it was done in the past. They consult parish groups and programs to see if there are any other events that would be in conflict with the picnic. This information will help them choose the best date, time and place.

Next, they decide what the picnic will look like, what games to play, what food to offer, what music and activities to include. This answers the question, *Where Are We Going?* Once these decisions have been made, the committee begins the implementation stage by dividing up the chores and assigning tasks to various groups and committees. They are now dealing with the question, *How Do We Get There?*

After the picnic is over, the planners gather to assess the event and to look at what worked and what didn't work and why. They are answering the question, *How Close Did We Come?* This evaluation will serve as useful information for next year's picnic. The cycle of planning is now complete and ready for the planners of next year's event.

During this process someone might ask whether the picnic should perhaps be a fund-raiser as well. This leads to the central question, the hub or focus of the planning process, *Who Are We?* When this question surfaces, the social committee discusses the issue and decides that the summer picnic is meant to build community in the parish and to provide an opportunity for people to enjoy themselves. The function of the picnic is not to raise money for parish projects. This helps committee members focus their energies throughout the planning process. It keeps them centered.

The planning cycle can also work for larger projects. Consider a parish that is in need of a new church building. The present structure can no longer accommodate the influx of new parishioners. The overcrowding at the Masses is clear evidence that something must be done and done quickly. Information gathering is the first stage that must take place in planning for a new church. Much more will follow, including the investigation of sites, costs, diocesan guidelines and possible models.

Perhaps at this early stage of planning someone will ask, "What is the purpose of a new church building?" It is at this moment that the question, *Who Are We?* can be addressed. Why have a church? What is its function? What should it help people do? The answers to these core questions help shape the design of the new church.

Once the community has clarified the purpose of the new building, then they can decide what the building will look like. There is an important distinction between *Who Are We?* and *Where Are We Going?* The first question deals with purpose, mission and core values and provides the bedrock for planning. The answers to *Where Are We Going?* are vision statements. These change as the circumstances, needs and expectations change. Visions and goals are not the same as mission. Visions change with the situation and people involved. Mission remains stable and is adjusted only when major shifts in values and purpose take place.

Once the vision of a new church is set, implementation follows. This includes raising money, getting bids, breaking ground and building the structure. When it is finished, the leaders and people evaluate how it fulfills the purpose for which it was built. Is it an adequate and fitting structure in which to give praise to God? Is it a fulfilling place for the gathered community to share worship and ritual?

The planning cycle can get bogged down at any stage of the process. Sometimes a group gets stuck in the information gathering stage.

It collects more and more data but never makes a decision about its future. This usually happens when influential members don't want to change, don't want to try out a new way of operating or are afraid of a new vision.

At other times, a group moves through the visioning stage (*Where Are We Going?*) but the plan is never implemented. This is because there is no ownership among those responsible for putting the plan into action. The planning cycle can also get bogged down in the evaluation stage. If people are unwilling or unable to evaluate what worked or didn't work, the cycle is not complete.

A planning group can also answer all the questions on the outside ring of the cycle and miss the purpose for their planning. The plan might not reflect the core values or purposes of the group or organization. A wedding ceremony, for example, might have good music, lovely attire and beautiful flowers, but something seems to be missing. The ceremony lacks "soul" or purpose.

This chapter, and the two that follow, are based on the five questions of the planning cycle. They provide work sheets and reflective exercises to assist leaders and people in the important task of pastoral planning.

WHO ARE WE?

St. Mary's is faced with a dilemma. Ten years ago no one thought of asking the question *Who Are We?* Everything was running smoothly. The area changed and now over half of the parishioners are of Hispanic, primarily Mexican, origin. It functions like two separate parishes, one that speaks English and one that speaks Spanish. What can be done to link the two groups together?

On the other end of the diocese, Blessed Sacrament is facing a similar dilemma. It was a rural parish serving a farming community. Then urban development moved in that direction. In the last few years the parish has become divided between "old-timers" and young, upwardly mobile commuters. This parish also has two diverse "cultures," one that speaks "small town talk" and the other that speaks "city talk."

In both situations, the effort to discover a common mission is paramount. One way to proceed is to look at spirituality. How well is the leadership of the parish fostering spiritual values among the people? Spirituality is not a simple notion. It includes three dimensions, *personal, relational* and *societal*.

On the *personal* side, one of the essential tasks of a parish is to assist people, both old and young, in developing their relationship with God. This includes opportunities for prayer, praise and thanks, asking forgiveness and assistance in times of need. It also includes care for one's body as a temple of the Spirit, discovering what direction to follow in life and the creative use of one's gifts and talents.

Helping people develop a personal side of spirituality is not enough. Parishioners need to be challenged to develop a *relational* side as well. So much of American society is individualistic. Helping people develop this aspect of their spirituality includes not only loving and caring for others, but the willingness to be loved and cared for by others. It includes opening up to the community, receiving direction from others, working with others to create something new. This relational side of spirituality also manifests itself in rituals and celebrations.

There is a third dimension to spirituality that is needed for a complete and integrated picture. Parish communities, if they are to be followers of Christ, must challenge their members to develop the *societal* side. This includes an openness to diverse cultures and ethnic groups, care for nature and support for the poor and oppressed. It is this societal aspect of spirituality that can help parishioners in the two situations mentioned earlier to discover that they are not two parishes but one church.

Work Sheet **6-A** provides a brief description of the three aspects of spirituality. It can be used as an outline for evaluating one's own strengths and areas of need. It can also serve as a help in discovering to what extent each area is being fostered in the parish as a whole. Work Sheet **6-B** can be used as a guide in this reflection.

Discovering the strengths and needs in fostering parish spirituality is one way of answering the question, **Who Are We?** In the Hispanic/Anglo parish, the staff and council identified core values despite the diversity of cultures. In the rural/urban parish, the leaders discovered a common theme of ecology and care for the earth that helped unite the parish.

The next step in locating the core purpose or mission for a parish is to uncover various models of parish present among the leaders and people. One way of doing this is to play the **Whatsit** game described in Section **6-C**. Each participant is asked to arrange a deck of cards according to what he or she thinks is essential to the parish. In groups of four to eight, people play their cards from most to least important. As they do so, they discuss similarities and differences found in the group. The results from each small group are gathered into one composite score. From this exercise it is possible to discover what aspect of parish is most important, whether institution, community, sacrament, herald or servant. Identifying these core models of parish takes the leaders and people one step closer to answering the question, **Who Are We?**

Another step in this direction is to articulate the mission of the parish. This is often done in a brief "mission statement" that summarizes what makes the parish or group unique. The work on forming a mission statement may not come at the beginning of a planning process. It is more effective if it is done when it becomes an important issue for the group. Too often people expend energy creating a mission statement only to put it on a shelf or in a picture frame and never refer to it again.

When, *Who Are We?*, becomes an issue, forming the statement does not need to take a long time. The following is an example of a mission statement for a pastoral council.

St. Edward's Pastoral Council is a faith-filled leadership body, guided by the Holy Spirit and the Gospel. It works in conjunction with the pastor and staff to discern the needs of the parish. By setting goals and priorities, it guides the parish in building a Christ-centered community of faith.

There are some basic elements that all effective mission statements should include. First, it should identify the group. In the above statement, the **Who Are We?** is described as a *faith-filled leadership body guided by the Holy Spirit and the Gospel*. Second, the statement should include the *function* of the group. For St. Edward's council, the function is both *to discern the needs* and to *guide*. A good mission statement should also describe *how* the group will accomplish this function. In the example, the pastoral council will do it by *working with the pastor and staff* and by *setting goals and priorities*. Finally, a mission statement should indicate the people *for whom* the group exists. In this case, it is *the parish community*.

Work Sheet **6-D** contains these four elements of an effective mission statement. It can help in both the formulation of a new statement or in the evaluation of one that already exists.

Work Sheets **6-E1** and **6-E2** provides an outline for helping a group formulate a mission statement based on scripture and core values. The statement could describe the parish as a whole, or any part of the parish.

If the leadership in either of the two parishes mentioned earlier had spent time trying to answer the question, *Who Are We?*, they would have uncovered a unique richness in the diversity of their people and their traditions. This, in turn, would lead to a new vitality and rebirth for their communities. Too often this core question is never asked. The result is confusion and ambiguity about what is essential to the life and future of the parish.

WHERE ARE WE NOW?

Let us return to our original example of the parish that was threatened with closing. The diocese agreed to assign a non-ordained pastoral administrator to the parish. The priest from the neighboring town would handle the Masses and sacraments.

The new administrator arrived last weekend and is trying to assess the situation. What is the parish like? What is its history? What are the people's needs and expectations?

Her first step is to call the leaders together for an evening of information gathering. She puts a large sheet of paper on the wall. After drawing a line across the paper, she asks people to identify the significant events in the life of the parish over the last twenty years, both high points and low.

What follows is half an hour of animated sharing of stories about the parish. The pastoral administrator has no trouble filling the paper with the names of key persons and events. A few of the memories that came flooding back into people's consciousness were the church renovation, the pastors who came and went, the fire in the rectory and the controversy over selling liquor at the summer picnic.

When the sheet is full, she asks everyone to think of a word or phrase that best describes the parish at the present time. These words are added to the sheet as well. Some examples include "at a crossroads," "hanging on," "ready for new birth," "confused," "feeling lost and abandoned," "on the brink."

This exercise prompts much discussion about the parish's history and present situation. By the end of the evening, the new administrator has a good sense of the parish, both past and present. (Work Sheet **6-F** provides a description of this information gathering technique.)

As people leave the meeting, the administrator passes out a work sheet to encourage reflection. Over the next two weeks the leaders are to think about all that is happening in the parish. They determine what aspects are in decline and which ones are alive or coming to life. [See Work Sheet **6-G**.]

At the end of the two weeks they return full of energy and ideas. In small groups, the leaders compare their responses and then gather as a single group to share their insights. The leaders agree that some areas of the parish have died, such as easy access to a priest and daily Mass. Other aspects are coming to life. There is a new sense of ownership among the people and a willingness to make this experiment of a pastoral administrator work. What is waiting to be born is a whole new way of being parish.

Within a month of her arrival, the administrator knew much about the parish, at least as it was experienced by the leadership. Does this match the parishioners' perspective? She had many options to follow to get the answer. Work Sheets **6-H1** and **6-H2** provide a checklist of information gathering alternatives. Some methods work better for small groups of three to twenty-five people. Other methods are more suited to larger gatherings or an entire parish community.

The pastoral administrator decides to start with the census. No one is sure when the last census was taken or whether the files are up-to-date. Using Forms **6-I1** and **6-I2** she asks every household attending church to fill out a registration update card. A few volunteers then match the cards with the census file to see who is not accounted for. These parishioners are contacted to see if they are still in the area and want to continue as members of the parish.

At the end of her third month, not only does the administrator know how the leaders size up the parish, she also knows how many people are members of the parish. What she does not know are their needs and desires. Rather than rely on the leaders' perceptions, she decides to ask the parishioners directly. She tells the people that she wants to do a survey of attitudes and asks volunteers to help in this project. A special committee is formed and, using the checklist contained in Work Sheets **6-J1** and **6-J2**, constructs a parish survey of attitudes. The committee sends it to a random sample of parishioners. Interest is so high that 65% send it back.

The committee goes to work processing the results and writing a report. This report is given to the leaders and a summary sent to the entire membership. Some of the results surprise the leaders, while others are close to what they had expected. They are surprised, for instance, that many people do not want more participation in parish decision-making. The leaders are *not* surprised to learn that a majority favored the new position of pastoral administrator.

As the leadership gathers to process the survey results, they realize that there is far too much information to handle all at once. They decided to focus the material and concentrate on just a few areas.

Using the prioritizing exercise contained in Work Sheet **6-K**, the administrator and leaders are able to identify the more pressing needs in the parish. Some of these needs include improving the music at Mass (especially the congregational singing), providing opportunities for parishioners to take an active role in running the parish, reaching out to the less active and marginal members, and increasing financial contributions to the parish.

In order to get the parishioners' reaction to the leaders' list of parish needs, everyone is invited to a special gathering after a Sunday morning Mass. The leaders present the list of needs and elicit reactions and comments. They also ask people to prioritize the needs and identify others that may be missing from the list. The leaders use the guidelines for town hall meetings contained in Work Sheets **6-L1** and **6-L2**. This experience stirs up much interest and excitement about what will be happening in the parish. This is the most enthusiasm anyone remembers seeing for many years.

Over the six months, the pastoral administrator's constant refrain has been; "What is the situation? What are we dealing with? What do the people want and need?" If the administrator had listened only to the leaders' impressions and insights she would have missed the important information from the surveys and town hall meeting. Not only did these exercises increase her awareness, it raised expectations among the parish community as well.

This is the mentality associated with the second step of the planning process that concentrates on, **Where Are We Now?** An accurate answer to this question sets the stage for the next step in the process which is, **Where Are We Going?** It is time to move on to the next stage of visioning and dreaming outlined in the next chapter.

ADDITIONAL RESOURCES

Baldwin, David, *Tomorrow's Parish, Choosing Your Future*. Chicago: Office of Research and Planning, Archdiocese of Chicago. 1993.

Balhoff, Michael, *Strategic Planning for Pastoral Ministry*. Washington, D.C.: The Pastoral Press. 1992.

Dulles, SJ, Avery, *A Church To Believe In: Discipleship And The Dynamics Of Freedom*. NY: Crossroads. 1982.

Handy, Charles, *Understanding Organizations*. NY: Oxford Press. 1993.

McKinney, O.S. B., Mary Benet, *Sharing Wisdom, A Process for Group Decision Making*. Allen, TX: Tabor Publishing. 1987.

Sweetser, Thomas and Patricia Forster, *Transforming the Parish*. Kansas City: Sheed & Ward. 1993. Chapters Three and Twelve.

SPIRITUALITY

Spirituality is a complex notion. It contains aspects that are **personal**, **relational** and **societal**. Using Work Sheet **6-B**, reflect on what are your own strong points and areas of need. How does the parish and areas of ministry exemplify these aspects? What are areas of need?

 PERSONAL

1. **Prayer** -- Has a personal relationship with God, is a person of prayer

2. **Praise** -- Gives thanks for nature and personal gifts, manifests joy in life

3. **Need** -- Aware of limitations, is not self-sufficient

4. **Response** -- Acceptance of God's graces, willing to change

5. **Fitness** -- Cares for oneself, makes time for leisure and exercise

6. **Direction** -- Has sense of purpose in life, motivated

7. **Creativity** -- Uses gifts and talents, inventive

8. **Reflection** -- Takes time to examine life, be quiet

RELATIONAL

1. **Interaction with others** -- Open to growth, interested in others

2. **Loving** -- Loving others and willing to be loved

3. **Caring** -- Ministering to the needs of others, empathetic

4. **Celebration** -- Knows how to ritualize, relate in symbols, song, poetry

5. **Community** -- Risks self-disclosure, is loyal, honest

6. **Direction from others** -- open to advice, spiritual counsel

7. **Generativity** -- Joins with others to make something new, is fruitful

SOCIETAL

1. **God's Involvement** -- Aware of God's work in creation and the world

2. **Protecting rights** -- Willing to work for justice, defend the powerless

3. **Working within structures** -- Able to fit into organizations, accept boundaries

4. **Prophetic** -- Willing to stand up and take a stand, challenging and forthright

5. **Overcoming prejudices** -- Aware of personal prejudices, admit weakness

6. **United people** -- Works to unite peoples and religions

7. **Care for nature** -- Treasures the earth, concern for ecology, conservation

6-A

ASSESSING OUR LEVEL OF SPIRITUALITY

Using 1-B as a guide, indicate your own areas of strength and need in each aspect of spirituality. Then reflect on your area of ministry and assess how well the three aspects of spirituality are being fostered among the people in that ministry, both areas of strength and need.

AREAS OF STRENGTH	AREAS OF NEED

PERSONAL

SELF

_____

_____

_____

MINISTRY

_____

_____

_____

RELATIONAL

SELF

_____

_____

_____

MINISTRY

_____

_____

_____

SOCIETAL

SELF

_____

_____

_____

MINISTRY

_____

_____

_____

●••Whatsit•••

A Game for your Parish: Staff, Council, Parish Groups

To Help Uncover Different Understandings of Church and Parish

PURPOSE

The purpose of WHATSIT is to help people see how they and others view the parish. In this card game a pastor or pastoral team plays the game with the pastoral council, men's or women's group, youth group or some other interested parish gathering, the more diversified the better, to determine what each believes the parish is or should be. This game will help people become aware of the different perceptions of parish in their group. (Approximate time: 1 hour)

PROCEDURE

1. Participants take their places around a table. No group should be more than ten people or less than four.

2. Participants are given an identical set of 12 cards, ten of which indicate a specific understanding or emphasis for the parish and two of which are blank. [6-C2] These blanks are used if a participant feels there are one or two ways of viewing the parish not given.

3. Participants are to arrange the cards from what they consider most important to least important. They put all twelve cards into one single deck. Allow five to ten minutes for this process.

4. When everyone is ready to play, the leader asks each participant to discard, face down in front of them, the five cards he or she considers the lowest priority. These five cards may or may not contain one or both of the blank cards.

5. Each participant, including the leader, turns over the top priority card indicating the *best* way to describe the parish or its operation. One player then reads his or her top priority card and indicates why this card was the most important. Discussion continues as long as there is interest. The participants read, in turn, the top priority card and discuss why it is so important. Whenever anyone turns up a blank card he or she indicates what aspect of parish should have been included and why. Then the second choice card is placed next to the first card and each person in turn discusses this priority. A different person starts each round of cards. After the group has finished with three cards, participants pause to see if there is a consensus or where differences exist.

6. After all of the hand-held cards have been played, the discards in front of each participant are turned up, examined and discussed. Each person explains why these priorities are less important than other aspects of parish life.

7. After this discussion, everyone picks up his or her original set of twelve cards and puts them in the order he or she now thinks they belong. This allows people to reorder their cards after listening to other ideas around the table. This time, seven cards of least priority are discarded. The remaining five cards are played one at a time. The number of each card is recorded on the score sheet for each round of play.

8. The score sheet is then tallied by giving each first choice card 5 points, second choice card 4 points, etc. until all choices are given a weighted value. The composite score for the group in each category is then placed at the far left of the score sheet.

9. Refer to the *Models of the Church* description sheet [6-C3] to see which models of parish received the highest score from the group. If more than one group is playing the game at one time, the scores from all the small groups are added together to determine the models of parish that received the most points from all groups combined.

Whatsit Cards

1. The most important work of the parish is to teach, sanctify and give direction for the moral lives of the parishioners.

2. The strength of the parish depends on the strong leadership of the pastor.

3. The most important work of the parish is to form a closer feeling of community among the parishioners.

4. The strength of the parish depends on the working of the Holy Spirit within and among the people.

5. The most important work of the parish is to celebrate the Eucharist and administer the sacraments.

6. The strength of the parish depends on a good liturgical program providing a variety of forms for worship.

7. The most important work of the parish is to proclaim the Word of God to parishioners.

8. The strength of the parish depends on how well the people listen and respond to the Gospel that is preached to them.

9. The most important work of the parish is to care for the people who are in need of help in the parish and neighborhood.

10. The strength of the parish depends on how well it becomes aware of and responds to areas of injustice in the community or in the world at large.

11. The most important work of the parish is:

12. The strength of the parish depends on:

WHATSIT

SCORE SHEET

Score	Parish As	Card No.	ORDER OF PRIORITY					Total	Combined Score
			1	2	3	4	5		
			# x 5 =	# x 4 =	# x 3 =	# x 2 =	# x 1 =		
	Institution	1.							
		2.							
	Community	3.							
		4.							
	Sacrament	5.							
		6.							
	Herald	7.							
		8.							
	Servant	9.							
		10.							
	**	11.							
	**	12.							

*Combined Score equals total of lines 1 and 2, lines 3 and 4, etc.

**Fill in, if needed.

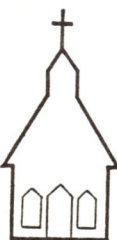

WHATSIT: MODELS OF CHURCH

WHATSIT is based on Avery Dulles' Models of the Church (NY: Doubleday, 1974). This sheet is intended to give a brief description of each model, with the understanding that no one model is the *correct* or best understanding of the Catholic Church or parish. All are necessary in order to maintain the rich diversity found in the Catholic Church today. These models are helpful to indicate a person's or group's emphasis about the Catholic Church or the parish. [See Avery Dulles' A Church To Believe In (NY: Crossroads, 1982) for a blending of these aspects into a model of discipleship.]

The Parish as:

INSTITUTION: This model stresses continuity with Catholic tradition and the importance of structure and order in the operation of the parish. There is a well-ordered distribution of responsibility with the pastor and priests as the focus of the parish. The important aspects of a parish from this perspective are the authority of the Church to teach and govern, a well-defined code of moral behavior and a set of guidelines for the administration of the sacraments and the celebration of the Mass.

COMMUNITY: This model stresses the presence of the Holy Spirit in the people gathered together to pray and worship the Lord together. The emphasis here is on forming a community and in sharing faith experiences together. Those who view the parish from this perspective are not as concerned about the structure of the parish or its operation as they are about how close the parishioners feel toward one another. The Spirit is manifested in the parish by the way the people work at building Christian community in the parish.

SACRAMENT: This model stresses the sacramental life of the parish as a sign or manifestation of Christ's presence. The Incarnate Christ is the emphasis in this understanding of the parish, in such a way that the parish seeks to carry on the work of Christ and celebrate His presence together in the Eucharist. The focal point for the parish is the Mass. An attempt is made to offer a variety of Mass styles so that as many people as possible are included.

HERALD: This model stresses the importance of the Word of God and the power this Word can have on the parishioners if it is proclaimed and preached as it should be. This view of the parish emphasizes Scripture and its application to the daily lives of the people. The parish comes to life when the Word of God is preached and the people receive it and make it operative, much like the power that the Word of God has in the Hebrew and Christian scriptures.

SERVANT: This model stresses the obligations of all parishioners to care for those in need, to heal and help the powerless, to work for peace, justice and the righting of wrongs in the local community and in the world at large. Here the emphasis is on action and service rather than doctrine, liturgy or parish gatherings. The bond that holds the parish together, according to this approach is the commitment all Christians make to care for their brothers and sisters. If they are hurting then the parish hurts also. The parish is healer.

Note: It may happen that a person or group of people will fill out a blank card with a unique understanding of the parish. An attempt should be made to see if it can be related to any of the five listed above and mark the score sheet accordingly. If this is not possible, then the discussion of this new approach to the parish should prove helpful.

ELEMENTS OF A MISSION STATEMENT

A Mission Statement should briefly summarize the purpose of a group or organization. From reading the statement, a person not familiar with the group will know what the group is about and what makes it unique. It serves as an articulation of the core beliefs and central focus of the group.

The following four elements should be contained in any Mission Statement. Use these four questions to critique and analyze a Mission Statement. If an area is missing, the group should explore ways for including it in the statement.

Does the Mission Statement provide information about:

1. ***Who Are We?***

    Examples: Called by God, led by the Spirit, followers of Jesus, in the Catholic tradition, pastoral team, faith-filled body

2. ***What Function Do We Have?***

    Examples: Form community, minister to people's needs, respond to changing situations, discern new directions, foster mutuality

3. ***How Do We Accomplish This Function?***

    Examples: Supporting each other, challenging people to grow, prayerful discernment, modeling partnership

4. ***For Whom?***

    Examples: Our community, those in need, ever-changing world, one another, the poor and marginalized, parishioners

PROCESS FOR ARRIVING AT A MISSION STATEMENT

Length: Three to four hours with option for final writing committee following the meeting

Number: Fifteen to twenty-five people

Materials: One bible for each person, about 15 large pieces of paper, markers, masking tape, optional taped music for prayer, index cards and pens or pencils for everyone

Process:

1. Set the mood with introductions describing the process and purpose of the meeting, i.e., to come up with a mission statement of **who we are** and **why we exist**.

2. Invite participants to prayer with introductory liturgical or meditation music and a scripture reading. The reading should set the tone or mood for individual bible reading and reflection.

3. After the reading, invite everyone to find a quiet place for reflection. Using the bible, look for a passage that describes **who we are** or **what we are called to**, i.e., passages related to discipleship, community, call or mission, etc.

4. Allow about fifteen minutes for the individual reflection and then call the people back to the large group. Ask people to share the theme of the passage they chose, to read one or two verses from the passage and describe what it meant to them. There should be no discussion at this point, only prayerful sharing. After all have had a chance to share their passage, ask the group for insights into common themes, important emphasis or key ideas and phrases. A summary of these insights should be listed on large sheets of paper for all to see.

5. Along with these insights from prayer, ask people to add to the list any other key words or phrases that help describe **who we are** or **our purpose** and reason for existing. Do this brainstorming without any discussion.

6. Once the list is complete, pass out one index card to each person and ask everyone to prayerfully look over the list of insights from the scripture passages and the brainstorming. Using this as a reference, each person is to construct a mission statement of **who we are**. This should take about five to ten minutes, everyone working on his/her own while studying the lists.

7. Depending on the number of people, break into groups of about four to five persons each. Invite each group to an experience of active listening. One at a time, each person reads his or her statement aloud and slowly. Everyone else listens intently, without comment. After everyone has read his or her statement aloud, go around the group again. Ask people to identify common phrases or words that people think are good to keep for one common statement.

8. Using the best ideas, phrases and insights from individual statements, each small group develops a group statement. Everyone in the small group should be able to accept it as representing their sentiments and feel good about presenting it to the large group.

9. The mission statement from each small group is brought back to the large group and everyone listens to each statement without comment. Once all the small group statements are read, pause for a moment, asking God's help in discerning what are the best aspects of each statement. Then read all the statements again and look for common themes, phrases and ideas in an effort to combine the statements into a single one.

10. It may not be possible to arrive at the final version during the meeting. In this case, one person from each small group is asked to volunteer to form a subcommittee to work out the final version. The entire group gives ideas to the subcommittee, acknowledging the best parts of each small group statement.

11. Once the subcommittee has come up with the final version, the original large group reconvenes to approve the mission statement. If the mission statement is for that particular group, such as the pastoral council or staff, then move to the next step of ratification. If your mission statement is for the parish as a whole, then this approved version goes to the parish community for reactions and feedback.

12. Once revisions are made and a final draft is approved, the statement must be ratified. This ratification could take the form of a prayer service in which the statement is divided up into subsections. One or two persons are called to reflect on that subsection and indicate what is implied by that section. At the conclusion of the reflections, the statement is read aloud by everyone in unison. While an appropriate song is played, everyone comes forward to sign his or her name. If it is a parish mission statement it might be used as a profession of faith at Mass or celebrated on a special feast day of the parish, etc.

13. Discuss how the mission statement can be used by the parish or group. Keep it visible. Perhaps it could be printed on stationery, the bulletin cover or on cards and read occasionally at Mass, etc.

WHERE HAVE WE COME FROM?

WHERE ARE WE NOW?

WHERE HAVE WE COME FROM?

One way of answering the question *Where Are We Now?* is to discover the significant moments in the group's past that led it to the present situation. One way of doing this is to construct a group *History Line*. This is done by drawing a line across a blackboard or large piece of paper.

SIGNIFICANT EVENTS IN THE LIFE OF _____

Year: _____   Present Moment

If the parish is the focus, then the line might start when it was founded, or perhaps twenty years ago. If a staff or council or other group is the focus, the line might start with the date of the person that has been there the longest. People are then free to add any items, persons, events or activities they can remember, along with the approximate dates. Events listed could be positive or negative, of recent memory (last week, last year, five years ago) or in the distant past (10 years ago or "at the beginning.")

WHERE ARE WE NOW?

Once all important items are on the history line, give each person an index card and ask people to write down a word or brief phrase that describes the group at this present moment. When everyone has written down the word, go around the group and have each person read the word or phrase. These are written on the board or on a new piece of paper to the right of the history line. Put a check in front of the ideas that are repeated. After all the words are listed, the leader reads the list for all to hear. People then give their impressions of how this describes the group or parish.

 REFLECTION QUESTIONS ON PRESENT SITUATION

What is **ALIVE** but **STRUGGLING**?

What is **DYING**?

What is **TOTALLY DEAD**?

What is **WAITING TO BE BORN**?

What is **BEGINNING TO COME TO LIFE**?

What is **FULLY ALIVE**?

INFORMATION GATHERING

There are many ways of gathering information about the present situation. Some methods are more appropriate for small groups (4 to 25 people). Other methods are better for larger groups and entire congregations. What follows are suggestions and options for both small and large groups.

SMALL GROUP SKILLS

1. **History line** of a person's experience in ministry, Church, parish, etc. (This is similar to Work Sheet **6-F**, but done with a focus on the personal history of each individual rather than on the group as a whole.)

2. **Weather report:** This can be done at the beginning of a meeting or whenever necessary. Ask each person what the "weather" is like inside: sunny, stormy, foggy, daybreak, etc. This provides information about people's dispositions and feelings that may affect one's involvement.

3. Use **index cards** for individuals to write down their reactions or insights into the topic or issue being discussed. The results are shared with those next to them or with the entire group. The cards may be collected for future reference.

4. **Brainstorm** with a group (preferably written on a board or large paper) so that people can get out ideas without worrying about being questioned or critiqued.

5. **Storytelling.** Let people tell their story about some important aspect of their lives (God, Church, Ministry, etc.) or about previous experiences in the group.

6. **Prayerful experiences** that give people the chance to share reflections on scripture or other readings and make petitions. This provides information about concerns and issues important to the participants.

7. **"I wish" cards**, where people can indicate what they would like to see happen at this meeting, in the parish, or with this group. It provides information about people's expectations and desires.

8. **Home visits**, either to individual homes or groups of families, so that parish leaders can learn what people would like to see happen in the parish and learn about areas of concern.

9. **Case studies or role-plays** where people have a chance to solve a situation in which they are not directly involved. Much information can be obtained from listening to how people solve the case studies or play fictitious roles.

10. **Brief interview sessions** following Mass as a way of obtaining feedback about the weekend homilies. Comments are written down or taped and then given to the homilist for reflection.

INFORMATION GATHERING

LARGE GROUP SKILLS

1. **Written surveys** with questions that have answers to choose from and questions that are open-ended [See Work Sheet **6-J1** & **6-J2** for suggestions.]

2. **Interviews**, both face-to-face and by telephone, using a structured format and uniform questions for easier tabulation and analysis

3. **Town hall meetings** or parish assemblies so the people can give reactions to parish policies and priorities [See Work Sheet **6-L1** & **6-L2** for ways of conducting town hall meetings.]

4. **Parish census**, both "in the pew updates" and door-to-door canvassing, that help keep parish files current and accurate [See Work Sheet **6-I1** & **6-I2**.]

5. A **Time/Talent search** or periodic requests for volunteers as a way of learning what people are willing and able to do in parish ministries and programs

6. A **"Message Card"** as a bulletin insert or in the pews where people check what programs or activities interest them (It can also include special needs they have or reactions to parish liturgies and functions.)

7. A **Welcome Wagon ministry** where newcomers to the parish have a chance to voice their desires and expectations for the parish (Not only is this a time to provide information to the newcomers, it is also an opportunity to learn about their skills, desires and previous experience.)

8. A **parish newsletter** that includes a tear out section for people to voice their opinions about some aspect of the parish (Suggestions can be mailed in or dropped in a suggestion box or the collection basket.)

9. Parish **"straw votes"** which carry no weight but give an indication of how people feel about an issue or pending decision (In this way people are consulted about important issues before a decision is made.)

10. **Priority Cards** where people can indicate first, second and third choices from a list of parish priorities or pressing needs (This information gives the leaders an awareness of what is of interest and concern to the people.)

11. **Sharing experiences** in preparation for a parish anniversary or celebration, information can be obtained as people relate their past experiences of the parish, group, etc. (This can be done in a structured format or informal gatherings.)

CENSUS UPDATE

Yearly Update

1. Once a year, or every other year, ask those who come to church to fill out a census update card. [See Form 6-12.] On a given weekend, one person from every household fills out the card immediately after the homily and drops it in the collection basket. For the next three weeks, households that have not filled out the card are reminded to do so. The best months to do this are October and March when most parishes have the greatest percentage of their people attending church.

2. A committee of volunteers matches the update cards with the parish census file, making whatever corrections necessary.

3. Households on the parish files for which there is no update card are contacted, either by phone or with a personal visit.

4. If there are many of these names, the parish might consider doing a special door-to-door census. This can also be an important evangelizing moment. Catholics in the area who have never registered in the parish are contacted, as well as those interested in learning more about the Catholic religion.

Door-To-Door Census

Assemble a special committee to organize the census. The tasks of the committee are as follows: (Some of these tasks can be done by subcommittees and support staff.)

1. Design a packet of materials that describes where the parish is located, what happens at the parish and what it has to offer.

2. Divide the parish into subsections and subdivide the sections into blocks that can be covered by a pair of canvassers.

3. Recruit leaders/captains for each subsection and call for volunteers to be parish visitors. Because this is a one-shot task which requires only one week of visiting twenty to thirty households, more people will be willing to participate.

4. Plan a training session before the canvasing begins and a follow-up session so that the canvassers can return their results and tell their stories.

5. Publicize the week-long event in the parish and surrounding neighborhood so that the community knows what is happening and is ready to receive the visitors. Those who have filled out an update card in church need not be visited, although this can be included as a courtesy and as a support to the parish visitors.

6. Information gained from the canvas is used to update the census file. Follow-up contacts are made to those who were interested or requested assistance.

CENSUS UPDATE FORM
Please Print

Address: _____ City: _____ Zip Code: _____

Mailing address if different: _____

Home Phone: _____ Work Phone: _____

Please write the first and last name of each person living at this address:	Date of Birth	Religion	Baptism	First Communion y/n	Confirmation y/n	Occupation / School
Adult's Name:						
Adult's Name:						
Minors:						
Additional Names:						

Would you like to have someone from the parish contact you? Yes _____ No _____

SUGGESTIONS FOR SURVEYING

Surveying can be an effective means of gathering information about the attitudes and practices of parishioners, whether it is the entire parish or subgroups within the parish. Care must be taken that the surveying is done well. The following questions are meant to help in this regard.

1. **Why are we doing this survey?**

    Is it to seek information? If so, continue with the rest of the questions. If, however, it is being used to tell people something about the parish or as an educational medium, use another means, not a survey.

2. **What are we looking for?**

    Is it to seek information about a specific aspect of the parish, such as liturgy, education, etc? If so, keep the questions within that focus. Is it information about the whole parish? Even in this case, try to have a clear focus about what you are looking for. The more focused the topic, the better the survey.

3. **How are we going to do the surveying?**

    There are a number of alternatives:

    a. Interviewing: This includes either face-to-face interviews or by telephone. This method provides personal contact but is more difficult to analyze. Telephoning is time-consuming, especially if many calls are required to make contact.

    b. Questionnaires: This includes questions that have multiple choice answers, open-ended questions with space for filling in answers or a combination of both. More people will respond to multiple choice questions, but open-ended questions provide added information not contained in set answers.

4. **Where are we going to do the surveying?**

    Interviewing: Face-to-face interviewing can be done by going door-to-door or by setting up interview areas, either individually or as a group (focus groups). If it is done by telephone, consider using multiple phone banks so that a number of people can be doing the phone interviewing at the same time.

    Questionnaires: The surveys can be mailed, given out at Mass, or distributed during a parish function. Caution: surveys given out at Mass do not reach those who do not come to Mass. People also tend to be more positive if they fill out surveys during or after Mass.

5. Who will be surveyed?

The information desired may come from a target group. In this case, survey just that group, such as parents of religious education children, people who attend adult education sessions, or those attending the 9:00 a.m. Sunday Mass.

Surveying the entire parish is more difficult. It is more accurate to survey a random sample of parishioners picked from the parish list than to send surveys to every parishioner. If there are 3000 adults in the parish, select 300 names at random and send surveys to this representative group. With a smaller number it is easier to make phone calls to remind people to return the survey. People also feel special if they are picked and others are not. It produces a higher response rate. This is true even for small target groups mentioned above.

6. What questions are we going to ask?

Whether it is an interview or a written survey, care should be used in constructing questions that are clear, simple, and neutral. First choose the areas to be examined, such as questions on parish Masses or programs. Break these areas into specific questions. Distribute the sample questions to a number of people for advice. Once the survey is in the final draft, give it to a few people as a pretest to see how well they understand and answer the questions. Locate sample questions and examples from outside resources to get ideas and use as models.

7. How are we going to tabulate the results?

Think about this **before** the survey reaches its final form. There are ways of constructing the survey and arranging the questions that makes tabulation much simpler. One hour spent in prearranging the survey saves ten hours in tabulation after the surveys are returned. Consider using a computer program to tabulate the results. The way the survey results are fed into the computer program may affect the way the questions are ordered on the survey. Work out these details **beforehand** because once the survey is sent out, no further changes can be made.

8. How are we going to write the report?

As was the case with tabulating the results, think about how the report of the findings will be written **before** the survey is distributed. Making comparisons between different groups is a good tool for reporting results. This includes comparing responses from men and women, different age groups, the active and inactive members, or last year's with this year's group, etc. If specific comparisons are desired, additional questions may need to be added.

Reference: The Parish Evaluation Project provides a do-it-yourself survey instrument and computer program for Catholic parishes called *INFORMED*. For information contact: 2200 E. Devon, Suite 283, Des Plaines, IL 60018. (847) 297-2080.

ESTABLISHING A HIERARCHY OF NEEDS

Instructions to group leaders:

1. Divide into groups of five to ten people each. Post a few sheets of large paper on the wall near each group.

2. Give each person in the group six (6) index cards.

3. Ask each person in the group to write down on the cards six **needs** they found in reading the survey report. (Focus on needs not solutions.) Have them answer this question on each card: "One need of the parish which has surfaced as a result of the survey is . . ." Only one need per card. Allow **ten minutes** for this. You take part in this process as well.

4. Go around the group asking each person to read **one** card. Summarize each item on the paper as it is read. Continue the process until all members of the group have read all six of their items, each in their turn. Many of the items will be repeated. In this case, place a check mark before the item on the paper to show that it was mentioned that many times in the group. This should take approximately **twenty minutes**. **Number the items** on the paper.

5. Give the members of the group **twenty minutes** to mill around the room to see what other groups have written on their paper. Encourage the members of your group to get as many ideas about the needs in the parish that other groups have indicated. (Use the back of the index cards.)

6. After consulting the other lists, reassemble your group and spend **ten minutes** adding to your list any **new** items that members of the group found helpful.

7. Next, give each member of your group **four** more index cards. Ask them to write on the cards the four most important needs on the list, one item per card. **No combining of items!** Allow **ten minutes** for this.

8. After they are finished, ask them to arrange the cards in order of importance, putting their first choice on top.

9. Now, go around the group asking each person to give their **first** choice. As the first choice is read, you write it on a new sheet of paper (briefly) and put a **4** after the item to show that it is the first choice and, thus, will get the most points (i.e., 4).

10. Continue the process until all four choices for each person are read, taking each person's second choice next, and so forth. Place a **3** after each second choice, a **2** after each third choice and a **1** after each fourth choice. State each item briefly. Many choices will be the same. In cases where an item is repeated, the appropriate number is placed behind that item depending on what choice it is for the person giving the item. The process should take **15 minutes**.

11. Finally, total up the number after each item and place the **total** points for that item in the left-hand column. The item that received the most points is the first priority for the group, and so forth.

12. Combine all the small groups' top priorities by adding the points together to form a single list of the most pressing needs from all groups. The entire process takes about **2 hours**.

SUGGESTIONS FOR PARISH TOWN HALL MEETINGS

PURPOSE: It is helpful to have periodic gatherings for the entire parish. Use these times to report on recent decisions or areas of planning, to gather information about important issues, to get reactions about future directions, and to provide visibility for parish staff and leaders. Care must be taken so that these gatherings are positive moments for the parish and not gripe sessions or shouting matches. They must also be well-planned and advertised so that people are interested enough to attend and feel good about the experience when they leave.

PROCESS:

1. Consider the reason for holding the gathering. If it is a regular event for the parish, it will need a special focus or purpose so that it stirs people's interest. If the gathering is to deal with a pressing issue facing the parish, provide opportunities for different opinions to be expressed in a way that others will hear and take into account.

2. Find a convenient time when people don't have to make an extra trip or hurry through a meal to get there. Try not to have the meeting when other important parish activities are taking place. Consider changing the Mass schedule to make room for the gathering. This also gives the meeting greater importance. Be sure child care is provided.

3. Begin by setting the mood or environment for creative listening and sharing. One way of doing this is to stress a climate of shared wisdom. Everyone present has a piece of the wisdom to share about the issue or topic to be discussed. Both in the way the room is set-up and in the demeanor of the leaders, people have a sense that they themselves are important and have something valuable to share.

4. Begin with a prayer that sets the mood for creative listening and sharing. Keep presentations interesting and limited in length. Consider a variety of methods for presenting material, including videos, overheads, role-plays, skits, anything that will maintain interest and still share the message.

5. Allow time for people to reflect individually on the material or presentation. Give them a chance to write down reactions or insights so that they will not forget their ideas as they listen to others speak.

6. Break into smaller groups in order to provide more opportunities for people to share their wisdom. If the group is large, these groups can be prearranged as people take their places around tables, or given a number on name tags. It is also possible to have people share ideas with those around them without having to move into groups.

7. Whatever the makeup of the small groups, creative ways should be found for obtaining information from each group. Rather than asking for a report, consider having each group make up a "Headline" on the issue discussed, or come up with a symbol or image of what they found important. Another option is to ask for only the one *best* idea from the group, or have a recorder write down the results to be brought to the leadership.

8. If people are given a chance to speak to the assembly as a whole, consider ways of limiting the comments and of keeping it positive in tone. For instance, if people want to speak, they have to say something positive before they can say anything negative. Curtail the talkers by limiting remarks to one minute, and be sure to enforce the rule early so that people know they cannot dominate the meeting.

9. Give people an incentive for coming to the meeting. This might include refreshments, handouts or articles, an occasion to meet new people, singing, having fun, a feeling of accomplishing something important for the parish community. Consider asking people to bring some refreshments that can be shared with others. This keeps people involved and invested in the meeting.

10. Publish the results soon after the gathering so that those who attended can see the results of their work and those who did not can see what they missed. Implement the results as well. Let people know that their efforts and concerns made a difference. They were heard and acted upon. It was a fruitful gathering, not an exercise in futility.

11. The more controversial the issues to be discussed, the more care that needs to be given to planning and running the meeting. Consider using an objective, outside facilitator for gatherings that include emotional topics and opposing sides. These gatherings can be positive moments for the parish, but only if care is taken to keep them interesting, creative and productive.

7 | PLANNING: VISION AND IMPLEMENTATION

"Without a vision, the people perish." (Proverbs 29:18) Knowing the present situation and current needs of the parish is only the beginning. Some decisions have to be made about the future, both short-term and long.

WHERE ARE WE GOING?

Once the leadership and people agree on the needs, something has to be done in response. If, in the example from Chapter 6, the Pastoral Administrator had gathered information and done nothing, the process would have died. Steps must be taken to move forward with a response.

Short-range goals and action plans help accomplish this. One way of proceeding is to use Work Sheets **7-A1** and **7-A2**. These pages describe a process for developing an action plan. Using the need of "providing opportunities for parishioners to take an active part in running the parish," the leaders imagine what the parish would look like if this need is met. Some of the ideals they come up with are: the people would take more ownership and participate in important parish decisions, they would attend parish gatherings, become involved in its programs and contribute more to the collection.

Next, the leaders list all that is going on now that encourages greater ownership by the people. Top on the list was the decision to confront the diocese and resist the closing of the parish. The parishioners took a stand and felt a sense of pride in their community. What more could be done to keep this spirit of involvement and ownership alive? The town hall following the survey report was another occasion for people to become involved in running the parish.

The leadership decides to have a gathering of the parish twice a year, once in the Fall and once in the Spring. The purpose of these gatherings will be to inform the parish about key decisions over the last six months and to ask ideas and direction for the next six months. A different format for each gathering will keep interest alive, including skits, role plays, small groups and videos. The leaders begin planning the first gathering to take place in three months. They decide to begin with a video presentation on transition. This short-range goal gives the leaders a concrete project to work on. It shows the people that the leaders are serious about responding to the priorities uncovered on the survey. To make sure they have arrived at a credible and productive action plan, they use Work Sheet **7-B** as a checklist. They agree that not only is this plan needed and realizable, it is also wanted by the people. The parishioners are more willing than ever before to participate in the future direction of the parish. The survey results proved this, as did the many informal comments made by parishioners before and after parish Masses and activities. The parish is on a roll.

The administrator is delighted by the initiative of the leaders. She also realizes that they will have to tackle the long-range side of planning. The diocese wants a plan from the parish within a year.

It is time to decide the bigger issues of whether the parish has a future and if so, what it will look like. Using the process described in Work Sheet **7-C**, the administrator calls a special meeting and challenges the leaders and people to envision the parish five years from now. What will be the "givens" in the parish at that time, the things that will not change but will influence the planning process? One "given," for instance, is that there will be no resident priest. People have to realize that a return to the "good old days" is unrealistic. Having a parish is not a "given," but having Catholics living in the town is.

Once all the "givens" are agreed upon, people gather around tables in groups of six to eight. The administrator asks each table to come up with the *worst* possible scenario for the community five years hence. When that is decided, each group is asked to construct the *best* possible scenario, one that fits within the boundaries of the "givens," but is as rosy a picture as the group can imagine.

Each small group then shares with everyone both the worst and best scenarios. Most of the worst ones describe the closing of the parish. The best scenarios are creative, including new buildings, programs and ministries.

The administrator then asks each group to come up with the most *realistic* scenario. This is the one that is most realizable, uses existing parish resources well and stays within the limits of the "givens."

The energy level is high as groups try to paint the picture of what the parish could look like in five years. As these realistic scenarios are shared with the assembly, common elements emerge. Each one includes pastoring by a pastoral administrator with a sacramental minister (priest) from outside. Each one also includes strong commitment and ownership by the people. They see the future as a partnership that includes lay leaders and the administrator together giving direction to the parish. A few of the people suggested expanding the scope of the parish. They hope that in five years the parish community will feel more secure and stable about its own future and devote more energy to the needs of the surrounding area. If all that is envisioned comes true, the parish could act as a guide and model to other parishes in the diocese that may face the loss of a resident priest.

People leave the assembly with energy and high hopes about the future of the parish. They have a sense that the future is in their hands, that they have some influence about what will happen to the community. They also praise the new administrator for her adept way of facilitating the process. She challenged them without controlling or pushing her own agenda.

Scenario building is only one of many ways to help a group envision its future. Another process is described in Work Sheet **7-D1**. Once people are in touch with their history and the present situation, they can dream about their future. Work Sheet **7-D2** provides an exercise for dreaming about key aspects of the parish: liturgies, activities, formation, outreach, leadership. After people decide where they want to be in three to five years, Work Sheet **7-D3** provides a means for translating the dreams into concrete action plans. If, for instance, a more inclusive and participative liturgy is the goal for worship, then one way of reaching this goal is to concentrate on congregational singing for the coming year.

Another approach to answering the question **Where Are We Going?** is the *Gonna-be* process contained in Section **7-E**. It is an attempt to stretch people's imaginations and get them thinking creatively about the future. It also helps sort out the difference between dreams that lead to long-range goals and those that lead to short-range goals.

Deciding where a group wants to go and what it wants to achieve is not an easy task. It requires good leadership and direction, as well as committed and motivated people. It is, however, an essential element for successful planning. "Without a vision, the people perish." They have nothing to shoot for, no dream or hope for the future. Of equal importance is planning ways for reaching the dream. This brings us to the fourth step in planning, implementation.

HOW DO WE GET THERE?

Implementing the dream is no easy task. It takes a variety of gifts and talents, approaches and techniques. The previous chapters have provided many helps and suggestions for "getting there."

The one area of implementation not covered by these chapters is the recruitment and matching of volunteers. If those who volunteer to help out with any activity or ministry are well-placed, both the community and the individuals who volunteer benefit. Work Sheet **7-F** contains four case studies in which the matching of volunteers to tasks was not done well. In the end everyone suffered. Using the case studies can be an effective means for learning how to recruit and care for volunteers.

The first step in effective recruitment is to define the tasks for which volunteers are needed. It is not enough to put a request for volunteers in the bulletin or make an announcement at the Masses. Even sponsoring a recruitment weekend at which people are asked to sign up for various jobs will not do it all. Parishioners need to know what is required, how much time it will take and how much background or experience is necessary. Work Sheet **7-G** provides a means for defining a task and what might be expected of the volunteer.

Once the task is defined, the next step is to discover the volunteer's gifts and inclinations. Work Sheet **7-H** provides a checklist for determining a volunteer's preferences.

The final step is to match the task with the volunteer. The care and sensitivity used in this placement process shows that volunteers are worthwhile and their needs and desires make a difference. It also results in better performance as people work at tasks they enjoy and find rewarding.

Once the person has been matched to a task or ministry, attention must be given to the care and development of the volunteer. Work Sheet **7-I** provides a checklist for recognizing the contributions of volunteers. The final chapter on evaluation resources provides a method for receiving feedback from volunteers when they complete a task or change ministries. [See Work Sheets **8-F1** and **8-F2**.]

HOW CLOSE DID WE COME?

Answering this question completes the planning cycle as people evaluate a project or ministry. They seek to discover what worked during the planning process and what failed. They also investigate the reasons *why* some things worked and others did not. This evaluation stage sets the scene for more information gathering, leading to new goals and methods of implementation. In this way, the cycle of planning never stops. There are always new situations and issues that require new directions and new ways of proceeding. The lasting values and core purpose of the group keeps the planning process focused. All else rotates around this central mission.

A further explanation of the evaluation stage of planning and associated work sheets are contained in the final chapter of this book.

ADDITIONAL RESOURCES

Bannon, William J., and Suzanne Donovan, S.C., *Volunteers and Ministry*. NY: Paulist Press. 1983.

Bausch, William J., *The Total Parish Manual*. Mystic, CT: Twenty-Third Publications. 1994.

Kouzes, James M., and Barry Z. Posner, *The Leadership Challenge, How To Get Extraordinary Things Done In Organizations*. San Francisco: Jossey-Bass Publishers. 1987.

Wilson, Marlene, *How To Mobilize Church Volunteers*. Minneapolis: Augsburg House. 1983.

RESPONSE PROCESS
Translating a Need into an Action Response

STEPS:

1. Choose one area of need to focus on.

2. List on paper the ideal we are working toward. In other words, if we had all the money, facilities, cooperation and staff we needed, if everything went right, what would this aspect of the parish look like in five years?

    Note: Use a "brainstorming" approach in which no one argues with another. If someone differs with what is put on the paper, they can put up something opposite to counteract that item. The intention is to get all the ideas and dreams out.

3. Try to find the common points in the ideal and dreams for the future so that everyone can agree this is what we are trying to accomplish and this is the ideal we want to achieve.

4. Next, list all the things going on in the parish that are helping us come closer to the ideal we just formulated. This is to affirm what we are already doing.

5. After listing all that we are doing now, ask people to "brainstorm" all the ideas and possible actions that could be initiated to reach the ideal. Don't worry about overlap or feasibility. Creative suggestions are what we want at this point.

6. The next step is to have the group look over the list. Choose **one** item that looks most promising at this time. This is the one (or ones, if some are combined) that is of interest to them or is the most possible.

7. Finally, take the Parish Action Contract Work Sheet **7-A2**. Apply the questions on that sheet to take care of the details in translating this one way of reaching the dream into a concrete action plan.

7-A2

PARISH ACTION CONTRACT

We of _____ Parish, commit ourselves to the following action:

_____
_____
_____
_____

It is directed to this group of people:

_____
_____
_____

It will happen at this time and this often:

_____
_____
_____

It will take place in these facilities or in this place:

_____
_____
_____

This group or these individuals will be responsible for the planning and continuation of this action:

_____
_____
_____

This is how this action will get started and stay in operation:

_____
_____
_____
_____

This is how we will measure its effectiveness:

_____
_____
_____

GUIDELINES FOR PARISH ACTION PLANS

7-B

One way of testing an action plan to see if it will be effective in an area of ministry is to apply the following criteria.

Is the Plan:

1. **NEEDED?**
   Is it something that will meet the needs of at least some of the parishioners, that is, is it constructive?

2. **CONCEIVABLE?**
   Can it be expressed in words and can people picture how it will happen?

3. **ACHIEVABLE?**
   Can it be done under the existing conditions and resources of the parish or area of ministry?

4. **BELIEVABLE?**
   Are the people involved in the planning of the parish or area of ministry willing to take this step or see it as possible?

5. **CONTROLLABLE?**
   Is it within bounds, or does it manipulate and force other people or groups without their consent?

6. **MEASURABLE?**
   Is there some way of telling that what you are attempting to do is or is not happening?

7. **WANTED?**
   Is this something that the staff, parish leaders and people want to have happen in the parish?

WORK SHEET FOR SCENARIO BUILDING

1. The process of **scenario building** is used to help groups envision the future. This work sheet can be filled out by an individual and the results shared with others, or it can be used as a guide for a group activity. The first step is to identify a **target date**. Next, establish the **givens** for that date. Once these have been agreed upon, then the individual or group paints the **worst** and **best** picture for that date. That leads to the most **realistic** scenario that lies somewhere between the best and the worst.

TARGET DATE: _____

GIVENS: These are the things that will not change. We have to work within the framework of these givens.

1. _____
2. _____
3. _____
4. _____
5. _____
6. _____
7. _____
8. _____
9. _____
10. _____
11. _____
12. _____

WORST: What do you see as the **worst** possible future for the parish or group? This is what might happen by the target date if we don't plan ahead.

_____
_____
_____
_____
_____

IDEAL: What do you see as the **ideal** future for the parish or group? This is what could happen by the target date if everything went perfectly.

_____
_____
_____
_____
_____

REALISTIC: What do you see as the most **realistic** future for the parish or group? This is what can happen by the target date if we use our resources well and plan ahead, being realistic but stretching ourselves as well.

_____
_____
_____
_____
_____

TRANSLATING DREAMS INTO ACTION
Process for Vision Workshop

STEPS:

1. Prepare the people for dreaming about the future by setting a prayerful, reflective environment. Pass out the Dreaming Work Sheet **7-D2** and ask each person to write down dreams and desires for each area of parish ministry. Ask people to write legibly because others will be reading these dreams. If they want to write on the back of the sheets, ask that it corresponds to the same area of dreaming as on the front of the sheets. This is because the sheets will be cut up into sections related to each area of ministry. Allow about 30 minutes for this personal reflection.

2. Collect the Dreaming sheets. Use a paper cutter to divide the sheets into six sections, one for each area of dreaming. Pile together all the dreams from each area.

3. Divide the people into six groups, one for each area of ministry: worship, community, education, outreach, administration, planning. Give each group the separated pages of dreams for that area of ministry.

4. Form the group into a circle and pass around the dreams for that area. Each person will have a few sheets to read. The dreams are read out loud, one at a time, going around the group until all the dreams are read. Ask the people not to make comments or notations are made as the dreams are read. The first time around only listen.

5. Go around a second time, asking people to summarize the central theme or gist of each dream they were asked to read. These core ideas are listed on large paper or a blackboard. The group is asked to pay attention for common threads and similar emphases.

6. Once the common themes are listed on the paper or blackboard, the group is asked to formulate a few goals that have surfaced from these dreams. These are long-range goals, that is, they should be desired outcomes that will provide direction to the parish for the next three to five years in the area of ministry under consideration. One to three goals are plenty to work on.

7. Once these goals are formulated, the group chooses one to concentrate on for the rest of the meeting time. A work sheet entitled **"What Do We Want To Accomplish In This Area?"** [7-D3] is passed out to the people. The participants fill in the spaces at the top of the sheet, listing the area of ministry under consideration and the goal that the group chose to work on at this time.

8. The group is then asked to brainstorm all the things that are now going on that are helping the parish come closer to this goal. These are listed on the board or on a new piece of paper for all to see.

9. After this list is completed, the people are then asked to answer the question: **"In light of this, where do we want to focus our energies for the coming year?"** These are ideas that will help move this area of ministry closer to the desired goal.

10. The people are then asked to develop actions to achieve this focus over the next six to twelve months. These ideas are listed on the board or paper. The leader should keep probing for creative ideas.

11. Once the people have all their ideas listed, the group decides who should be responsible for taking care of this action step and how to get started.

7-D2

PARISH VISION WORK SHEET

As I reflect on what I would like to see parish ministry look like by (year) _____, this is what I envision:

1. This is the way the parish worships and prays . . . (Describe your desired outcome (goals) for parish Masses, prayer experiences, spirituality, etc.).
_____
_____
_____
_____

2. This is the way the parishioners relate to each other . . . (Describe your desired outcome (goals) for community-building, activities, parish groupings, etc.).
_____
_____
_____
_____

3. This is the way the people, old and young, learn about their faith/tradition . . . (Describe your desired outcome (goals) in education for all areas and ages).
_____
_____
_____
_____

4. This is the way the parish relates to the larger community. . . (Describe your desired outcome (goals) for outreach, service, pastoral care, ecumenism).
_____
_____
_____
_____

5. This is the way the parish is managed . . . (Describe your desired outcome (goals) for use of resources, communication, staffing, decision-making, etc.).
_____
_____
_____
_____

6. This is the way the parish gets involved and plans for its future. . . (Describe your desired outcome (goals) for volunteers, newcomers, planning, etc.).
_____
_____
_____
_____

IF YOU USE THE OTHER SIDE, WRITE IN THE SAME POSITION AS ON THE FRONT.
Please write so that someone else will be able to read it.

7-D3

WHAT DO WE WANT TO ACCOMPLISH IN THIS AREA OF OUR PARISH?

AREA: _____

What do we want to accomplish by _____? _____

_____
_____
_____
_____
_____

What are we already doing that is helping us get there? _____

_____
_____
_____
_____
_____

In light of this, where do we want to focus our energies in the coming year? _____

_____
_____
_____

Action To Be Taken:	Who's Responsible:

●••Gonna-be••●

PURPOSE:
- To share dreams in each area of parish life
- To determine which dreams contribute to long-range goals and which to short-range goals
- To set long-range goals for specific areas of ministry

PROCESS:

1. Prepare the group for dreaming by creating a prayerful, reflective environment.

2. Give each person four 3 x 5 inch index cards. Ask them to write down four dreams about the parish that could take place five years from now. Write one dream per card. These dreams need to be written so that someone else can read them.

3. Once they have done this, ask them to indicate on the back of each card whether the dream is in the area of **worship, community-building, education, outreach,** or **leadership** (including staffing, council, administration and finance.)

4. Collect all the cards and shuffle them. Divide into small groups of four to seven people each and have them sit around tables. Place the *Gonna-be* board [7-E2] in the middle of the table. (The board can be enlarged for easier reading.)

5. Divide the dreaming cards into equal decks so that each small group has a deck. Tell the people to keep the cards in one deck, face down on the table. One person takes the top card, reads it out loud and places it on the board where he or she feels it belongs. This indicates whether the person feels the dream is likely to happen in the coming year, two or three years from now, four or five years from now, more than five years from now, or it will never happen.

6. Group members have one minute to try to change the person's mind if they disagree with the placement. After one minute, the individual makes a final decision whether to keep the card where it is or move it to another box.

7. The next person takes the second card from the deck and follows the same procedure. The game continues until all the cards have been read and placed on the board.

8. Once all the cards are read, those that were placed in the **Never** box are rewritten by the group so they can be placed in one of the other boxes.

9. Before removing the cards from the board, each card is given a number on the front of the card that fits the box in which it was placed, i.e., 1, 2-3, 4-5, 5+.

10. Those sitting around the table now remove the cards and rearrange them according to the categories listed on the back. All the worship cards go together, all the education, etc. If more than one category is listed, the group decides where it belongs.

11. The entire group reassembles and the cards from each small group are combined into five decks, one for worship, one for education, etc.

12. The cards are given to those responsible for coordinating and planning each area of ministry. They separate the cards into two piles. One pile contains dreams for the next three years. These contribute to short-range goals. The other pile contains dreams four years and beyond. These lead to long-range goals.

13. Taking the dreams from four years and beyond, they formulate one or two goals that will be accomplished in the parish five years from now. They also determine the action steps that will be taken for reaching these goals. [See Work Sheet **7-D3**.] This can happen as part of the meeting or be done at a later date.

WHEN IS IT . . . GONNA BE?

Within A Year

Event is likely to occur within a year

Within A Year

2 - 3 Years

Event is likely to occur in two to three years

2 - 3 Years

4 - 5 Years

Event is likely to occur in three to four years

4 - 5 Years

More than 5 Years

Event is likely to occur in five years

More than 5 Years

Never

Event is likely to never occur

Never

7-E2

VOLUNTEER CASE STUDIES

These situations provide practice in dealing with issues related to recruitment and care of volunteers. Divide into groups of three to six people. Each group tries to solve the problem related to one of the case studies and brings the results back to the large group. Another option is to have more than one group work on the same situation and compare the results.

CASE STUDIES

1. How do you deal with a woman who volunteers for everything? If a call goes out, she's there. The only difficulty is that she has a need to be needed. One wonders if her husband and children ever see her. She also tends to be overbearing. If she doesn't get her way, she takes it out on everyone else. Saying no to her is sometimes harder than having her part of the project. Most recently, you sent out an appeal for greeters at Mass and she, of course, volunteered. Unfortunately, she's just the person that should not be a greeter. If people see her at the main door they find another way to enter the church. Her involvement in the project is causing such strain that the whole thing may go under. What would you do to solve this problem?

2. The music director is the staff person who resources and facilitates the liturgy committee. He has his own way of operating and has his own opinions about liturgy. It is beginning to look like music is not only important, but the only focus of the weekend Masses. This is causing frustration among members of the liturgy committee who volunteer their time. They are now listeners to the music director's plans rather than co-planners of liturgies. Some of the best people have already stopped coming. If you confront the music director with this problem, he gets defensive. Getting into a funk, he plays mostly somber music for the duration of his mood. What would you do to solve this problem?

3. Two months ago the parish community life committee did a time-talent survey of the parish. They uncovered many new people who wanted to help out in the parish. It's now two months since the survey happened. People are beginning to telephone the office. Not hearing anything, they are wondering if the parish still wants their services? The community life committee is led by a wonderful person, but she has a hard time getting her act together. The rest of the committee has taken on the same attitude. They seem to be working hard, but there is nothing to show from their efforts. Urging them to contact those who volunteered seems to do no good. They just say they are working on it. What would you do to solve this problem?

4. You have a great bunch of CCD teachers, all except one. He's a nice enough guy, but he's behind the times. However, the kids love him. He plays games with them and tells stories. They have great fun. His class is the best attended. The only trouble is that his theology is pre-Trent. His focus is on the Baltimore catechism, which he has the children memorize. Little or nothing is said about the carryover of religion to Christian service and social awareness, although this is one of the stated goals of the religious education program. He can't be fired because the parents would be up in arms. You are not sure you can allow this situation to continue. What would you do to solve this problem?

7-G

JOB DESCRIPTION SHEET

This sheet provides a uniform way to describe tasks and ministries that require volunteers. Those seeking help complete the sheet so that a person interested in volunteering knows what might be expected, the type of task, what is required and how much time it will take.

AREA OF MINISTRY _____

NAME OF THE JOB _____

JOB DESCRIPTION _____

_____

_____

LOCATION OF JOB _____

DAY OF WEEK/TIME OF DAY _____

NUMBER OF HOURS PER MONTH _____

SKILLS REQUIRED _____

AMOUNT OF TRAINING NEEDED _____

MEETINGS REQUIRED _____

PERSON IN CHARGE_____

IF INTERESTED, CONTACT _____

PHONE _____

TYPE OF JOB (An X on the line describes the focus of the task. A mark close to the middle indicates it is a combination of both.)

WORKING ALONE _____ WORKING IN GROUP

LEADING OTHERS _____ FOLLOWING OTHERS

MUCH PREPARATION _____ LITTLE PREPARATION

DEFINED TASK _____ UNDEFINED TASK

SPECIFIC SKILLS NEEDED _____ NO SKILLS NEEDED

PERSONAL PREFERENCES OF VOLUNTEERS

7-H

Check all statements which you believe apply to you. This information will help decide what kind of volunteer ministry might be of interest to you.

1. __ I prefer to work alone.
2. __ I prefer to be a leader.
3. __ I prefer simple, routine tasks.
4. __ I prefer informal fellowship.
5. __ I prefer to do whatever is needed.
6. __ I prefer to work with people I know well.
7. __ I prefer a lot of responsibility.
8. __ I prefer to be known as skillful and intelligent.
9. __ I prefer to be liked by others.
10. __ I prefer a job that does not require much participation.
11. __ I prefer to see concrete results from my work.
12. __ I prefer to work on a small task or problem.
13. __ I prefer a job where I can witness to my faith.
14. __ I prefer a job which is visible and known by others.
15. __ I prefer to know what is expected of me.
16. __ I prefer to be part of a group.
17. __ I prefer to follow.
18. __ I prefer challenging new projects.
19. __ I prefer tasks with a clear assignment.
20. __ I prefer a job that is important, respected.
21. __ I prefer an opportunity to meet and get to know new people.
22. __ I prefer only a little responsibility.
23. __ I prefer to be known as friendly and caring.
24. __ I prefer to achieve something significant.
25. __ I prefer a job I can prepare for by reading and doing homework.
26. __ I prefer smooth, harmonious relationships.
27. __ I prefer large problems facing the community and the world.
28. __ I prefer a job which will be appreciated by my closest friends.
29. __ I prefer to try new things and redesign the job to fit me.
30. __ I prefer a job which will make my community a better place for the powerless and disadvantaged.

Adapted from "Volunteers and Volunteer Ministries", pg. 52, a booklet in <u>The Ministry of Volunteers, A Guidebook for Churches</u>. © 1979. Office for Church Life and Leadership, United Church of Christ, Cleveland, OH. Used by permission.

REWARDS AND BENEFITS FOR VOLUNTEERS

People volunteer for different reasons. Some are looking for companionship and affirmation. Others are seeking to accomplish a task and achieve success. Still others want to make a difference and have an impact. As a result, some types of rewards will be appreciated and valued by one person more than by another. Listed below are various ways of providing rewards and benefits for volunteers. Use the ideas as a checklist for recognizing the contributions of volunteers.

1. WAYS OF PROVIDING AFFIRMATION

- _____ Put names of volunteers in the bulletin or newsletter
- _____ Have a celebration, special Mass or party for volunteers
- _____ Put pictures of volunteers in prominent places
- _____ Provide pins and certificates for given years of service
- _____ Send cards on birthdays and special anniversaries
- _____ Have refreshments available at meetings and during tasks
- _____ Publicize the work of volunteers in local and diocesan newspapers
- _____ Create a conducive environment for sharing and getting to know people
- _____ Have name tags at larger gatherings so volunteers learn people's names
- _____ Provide gifts and mementos at Christmas or on other occasions

2. WAYS OF REWARDING ACHIEVEMENT

- _____ Budget extra money for new projects that reflect volunteers' ideas
- _____ Give people the tools and resources to expand their work
- _____ Ask volunteers for reports and feedback on the task
- _____ Encourage volunteers to explore new ways of doing a task
- _____ Provide child care while people are doing their tasks
- _____ Have resources available if people want to learn more about the task
- _____ Include the volunteers in the planning of the task or event
- _____ Give additional responsibility to the "veteran" volunteers
- _____ Write thank you notes for jobs well done or extra time spent on the task
- _____ Provide occasions for volunteers to assess their achievements and growth

3. WAYS OF ASSURING MEANING AND INFLUENCE

- _____ Show the volunteer how the task fits into the larger picture
- _____ Have the "veterans" train the new volunteers for a task
- _____ Have "volunteer ministry" as a theme at the weekend Masses
- _____ Provide occasions to share experiences with other volunteers
- _____ Challenge volunteers to grow and develop personally from the task
- _____ Provide scholarships for volunteers to attend workshops and classes
- _____ Acknowledge outstanding projects or achievements
- _____ Make spiritual direction available for those seeking personal growth
- _____ Ask people to talk about their volunteer experience at the weekend Masses
- _____ Form volunteer support groups for people to share joys and concerns
- _____ Keep the task interesting and as free from boredom and routine as possible

8 | PLANNING: EVALUATION – LINKING PAST PRESENT AND FUTURE

INTRODUCTION

The Easter Vigil started beautifully. The blessing of the fire took place in the side yard and all processed to the front of the church led by the light of Christ. The servers started up the steep stairs. They were each carrying the large candles used to help spread the light. Then it happened! One server tripped on his robe, falling forward. He caught the heals of the server in front of him, she too went flying and ended up with a bloody nose thanks to the marble banister. What a sight! Unfortunately, the same thing happened last year.

The word *evaluation* sends shivers down the spine of most God-fearing, job-loving people. This is most unfortunate. Evaluations are treasures waiting to be discovered. Whether it is a program, a ministry, a group or an individual, evaluations are the link between what we say we are about and how we are really doing. Evaluations are the keys to a successful future because they unlock the wisdom of the past.

COMPLETING THE CYCLE

Remember the Planning Cycle from Chapter Six? (If not, take a minute to look it over now.) We examined the first four steps in detail, but left the last step, "How close did we come?" for now. Since the Planning Cycle is indeed, a cycle, we cannot look at the end without being drawn back to the beginning. Who are we? What were we trying to do? How did we get to where we wanted to go? These questions are all part of the evaluation process. Reflecting on these broader elements sheds a new light on how evaluations can be used.

PRINCIPLES FOR EVALUATION

If evaluations have such multi-faceted benefits, then why is it we dread them so much? Most of the time it is the poor experiences of the past that feed these fears. Maybe this sounds familiar:

> I'm the DRE and my contract year was finished two weeks ago. I dropped another note to the Pastor asking that we get together for my evaluation. He is very busy but found time on Friday afternoon. We spent the first 20 minutes talking about the Easter liturgies. Eventually, he said that he was glad all is going well in my department. At least he hasn't heard any complaints. (At this point we were interrupted by a phone call.) Ten minutes later he returned and said I could expect the annual cost of living raise. On the way out the door he questioned why I had not done more with a Children's Liturgy of the Word program like St. Anne's, our

neighboring parish? (This was the first I had heard of this interest.) Before I could answer, another staff member grabbed him to ask a question and he was off....

This may or may not seem like an extreme case, depending on your own personal experiences. But it does surface some of the basic elements of evaluation that are necessary to make these experiences positive for all. What might an effective evaluation process look like? Imagine this possibility:

- It is the "tradition" of our community to evaluate everything on a regular basis.
- *Regular*, means that we have a set time of year to do each particular evaluation. In this way it is not a surprise to anyone or a practice used only when something goes wrong.
- Everyone knows ahead of time what will be included in the evaluation. This is because it is based on the person's job description or the predetermined goal or mission of a particular program.
- Information for the evaluation comes from those involved in leadership as well as those effected by the ministry.
- Strengths, and areas of growth, are discussed.
- Self-assessment and job satisfaction are part of the process.
- The evaluation session concludes with a brief summary of the meeting, noting new insights and next steps for the future.

Of course various elements of the process take on greater significance depending on whether you are evaluating an individual, a special event or a ministry. The central question becomes, "Do we value this person, event or ministry enough to take the time and energy needed to do an effective evaluation?" It is easy to answer *"yes, of course,"* but doing it is something else.

Like many things that are "good for you," getting into the habit of doing evaluations takes discipline. If evaluations are valuable, then reflecting on how they are actually done can lead to improving the process. Work Sheet **8-A** can be used to examine the evaluation process currently in place and consciously make choices about what is needed for the future.

EVALUATING INDIVIDUALS

In the earlier scenario, the DRE made an attempt to get feedback on her position. Unfortunately, she walked away from the experience disappointed and confused. In fact, the pastor too was frustrated. He wanted to give her more time and feedback but his schedule just would not allow it. How could this have been a better experience for both of them?

As we said earlier, evaluations do not exist in a vacuum. They are part of the larger planning cycle. *"How close did we come?"* is closely linked with *"Who are we?"* In parish staff situations, this can often be a difficult question to answer. The written job descriptions never really encompass all that is involved. Roles overlap, change, and multiply as programs are developed. We struggle to cover as many bases as possible. With regular reviews of what each person is doing, these traps can be avoided. Work Sheet **8-B1** can be used to reflect in detail on what an individual is already doing, and the level of satisfaction with each item. Because most staff members work closely with others and there are often overlapping roles, it is helpful to do this exercise as a group. Work Sheets **8-B1** and **8-B2** can be used together to answer the question, *"Who are we?"* for the entire staff. A suggested process for this is given on the next page. Adjustments can be made according to your needs.

A process such as this gives an individual feedback from their co-workers. This is one perspective. Those who work with the individual on a volunteer basis and those served by the minister also have insights to share. Work Sheets **8-C1** and **8-C2** provide a way of gaining information from these sources. To use these sheets, insert the name of the ministry (e.g. Music Minister, Principal, Social Justice Coordinator, etc.) on the blank lines. Work Sheet **8-C3** lists suggestions that may be used for evaluating the ministers performance, attitude, availability, etc. This list is just to get you started. Alternate questions may be appropriate depending on the individual's specific responsibilities.

EVALUATING MINISTRIES

Many of the principles for evaluating individuals can be applied to the groups and programs that comprise the community. It is not uncommon to expend much time and energy developing mission statements and long-range goals. These statements are very important to have. They can give a group a sense of direction and purpose. Yet, if they are neatly filed away and never used to review the group's progress, what purpose have they really served?

Like evaluating individuals, ministries can be evaluated by many different people: those served, those who work in the ministry, those who lead, etc. Each group will provide different pieces of

> **JOB DESCRIPTION PROCESS**
>
> 1. Fill out your individual job description sheet stating all items you handle, your level of satisfaction, and whether or not you are the ideal person to handle this.
> 2. Fill out the role description sheet for the other staff members.
> 3. One person volunteers to talk about his/her role. Put this person's name at the top of a large piece of paper.
> 4. Write down all the things *other* people listed under "What this person is doing now." (Use a black marker.)
> 5. The individual then comments on items others put on the list but he/she doesn't have on his/her list. (Star (*) these items, they are potential areas of confusion.)
> 6. The individual now adds to the list from his/her own paper. (Red marker)
> 7. Mark with a plus (+) the items that cause the greatest satisfaction. (Blue marker)
> 8. Mark with a minus (-) the items that cause the least satisfaction. (Blue marker)
> 9. Mark the items they would like to give away with an arrow. (Blue marker) Write on the arrow the name of the person or group who would be best to handle this item.
> 10. Write down all the things other people listed under "What do you think would be the ideal." (Green marker) A discussion follows between the individual and the group concerning changes for the future. (It may be that no one should be doing it.)
> 11. The next person becomes the focus. This process is repeated until the jobs of all members are addressed.
>
> After the exercise is complete, type all pages and give copies to everyone. In the end, each person will have a much better idea of what everyone else is doing, what brings them greatest satisfaction and how they can grow in the future.

information. Work Sheet **8-D** can be used by the group leading a ministry to evaluate progress. This exercise will reveal differing visions of the ministry and may help uncover underlying tensions plaguing the group. Reflecting on these questions results in a more life-giving, unified future together.

A practical aspect of group interaction involves time spent together in meetings. Nothing is more draining than meetings that seem to go on forever with no purpose. In Chapter 1, Leadership and Management, we discussed four important aspects of leadership: Environment, Leader, Group, S(s)pirit. All play a part in a group's effectiveness. Work Sheet **8-E** allows group members to rate these areas and make suggestions for improving the time spent together. Besides the valuable information gained, a greater feeling of ownership can be developed when this review is done by a group rather than one or two individuals. In addition to the leadership, there is another group of people who have much to tell us about our ministry and how it is working. These are the volunteers.

Volunteers have a unique perspective on a group. These people are usually in a group for a defined period of time. They see things as they are today. Yet, volunteers often feel unappreciated. They work *in the trenches*, meaning they see many weak points in the system. Work Sheets **8-F1** and **8-F2** provide a format in which volunteers can share their insights. Information from these evaluations can be used to shape training programs, to develop support structures and provide ongoing education. Because of their unique perspective, volunteers can raise issues that leaders may never have considered. Beyond evaluating group interaction, the activity of the ministry must also be evaluated.

Most groups or ministries have ongoing activities and projects. These are adjusted day-by-day as situations arise. What about those events which do not happen regularly? Remember the story from the beginning of the chapter? Everyone involved in the planning of the Easter Vigil remembered the incident from the year before, but not until it was too late. After a big event is finally completed, and the last bin of trash hauled away, the tendency is to move on to other things. What can be lost is all the wisdom gained from this experience, wisdom that would be very helpful next time this event takes place. Work Sheet **8-G** provides an outline for holding on to this information. It does not have to be lengthy, just a few notes, but the information will be very useful in the future. What worked well? What needs to be changed? Who was in charge of what? Where did the materials come from? How much did it cost? It's all there when planning starts again next year.

CONCLUSION

This brings us back to the core reason for evaluations: learn from the past to improve the future. As the saying goes, *"those who do not learn from the past are destined to relive it."* Communities are constantly changing, our people come and go. A tradition of doing evaluations provides the means for staying in touch with the changes and moving forward educated by experience.

PLANNING SUMMARY

In the last three chapters we have attempted to show that planning is not a luxury. It is a necessity. This is especially true for parishes facing limited personnel and resources. Handling crises on a day-to-day basis is neither effective nor healthy. Parishes must plan ahead and be ready for what they will be facing in the future. If they fail to do this, they will be at the mercy of impending conditions and circumstances. However, with careful and effective planning, they can shape their future and be prepared for what it may offer.

ADDITIONAL RESOURCES

Migliore, R. Henry, Robert E. Stevens, David L. Loudon, *Church and Ministry Strategic Planning, From Concepts To Success.* NY: The Haworth Press. 1994.

8-A

REVIEWING THE EVALUATION PROCESS

Read through these principles of evaluation. Reflect on how they are or are not used in your groups' evaluation process. Put a plus (+) by those you are already doing well. Put a minus (-) by those you are not using at this time. After personal reflection, discuss the results in a larger group and what could be done to make your evaluation process more effective.

EVALUATING INDIVIDUALS

___ Evaluations are done on a regular basis

___ Evaluations are based on a person's job description

___ Evaluations include time for giving support and acknowledging gifts

___ Evaluations provide clear expectations for areas of improvement including timelines for progress

Input comes from:

___ others involved in the person's ministry

___ those served by the minister

___ person or groups to whom the person being evaluated is accountable

___ a self-assessment by the person being evaluated

EVALUATING GROUPS AND MINISTRIES

___ Evaluations are done on a regular basis

___ Evaluations are based on a mission statement or goals

___ Adjustments made in goals for the following year are based on information learned in the evaluation

Input comes from:

___ leadership of group or ministry

___ others involved in the group or ministry

___ persons or groups served by the group or ministry being evaluated

8-B1

JOB DESCRIPTION

Complete the job description by stating all the items you handle (these things may or may not be reflected in your formal job description). Items can range from everyday tasks to once-a-year events. Next, mark your level of personal satisfaction with each item (**low, medium or high**). Finally, indicate who is the ideal person to handle this area. It might be you, it might be another staff person, pastoral council, parishioner, other or maybe no one should be doing this.

Item (What I Do)	Satisfaction	Ideal Performer
1.		
2.		
3.		
4.		
5.		
6.		
7.		
8.		
9.		
10.		
11.		
12.		
13.		
14.		
15.		
16.		
17.		
18.		
19.		
20.		
21.		
22.		
23.		
24.		
25.		

8-B2

ROLE DESCRIPTIONS

Fill out the role description box for three other staff members. (Perhaps each person can take the three sitting to his/her left.) In the space on the left, write down what you think each person is currently doing. In the space on the right, write down what you think would be ideal for each person. (What they might do to better focus energy, item to give up or pass on, or what more needs to be done.)

What this person is doing now: **What do you think would be the ideal:**

Name:_____

Name:_____

Name:_____

8-C1

FEEDBACK ON THE _____

You have been randomly selected from our parish to give your opinions and insights into the ministry and leadership of the _____ . This survey is anonymous so there is no need to include your name. Please return this form to the parish once you have finished. All envelopes will be given to an evaluation committee for analysis and reporting. The purpose of this survey is to let me know how I may better serve the needs of our parish community.

In Christ,

INSTRUCTIONS

Circle the number at the right of each question that corresponds to your rating of the _____ in the area mentioned. Mark only **one** number per question. If you want to make comments or explain any one of your responses, use the space beneath each question or an extra sheet of paper if you need more room.

1 = Excellent   2 = Good   3 = Fair   4 = Poor   5 = No Opinion

How do you rate the _____ in these areas?

1. _____ 1 2 3 4 5

2. _____ 1 2 3 4 5

3. _____ 1 2 3 4 5

4. _____ 1 2 3 4 5

5. _____ 1 2 3 4 5

6. _____ 1 2 3 4 5

7. _____ 1 2 3 4 5

8. _____ 1 2 3 4 5

9. _____ 1 2 3 4 5

10. _____ 1 2 3 4 5

11. _____ 1 2 3 4 5

12. _____ 1 2 3 4 5

13. _____ 1 2 3 4 5

14. _____ 1 2 3 4 5

15. _____ 1 2 3 4 5

16. _____ 1 2 3 4 5

17. _____ 1 2 3 4 5

18. _____ 1 2 3 4 5

19. _____ 1 2 3 4 5

20. _____ 1 2 3 4 5

21. _____ 1 2 3 4 5

22. _____ 1 2 3 4 5

23. _____ 1 2 3 4 5

24. _____ 1 2 3 4 5

25. _____ 1 2 3 4 5

26. _____ 1 2 3 4 5

27. In your opinion, what is the _____ greatest asset?

_____

_____

_____

28. In your opinion, what is one thing that would improve his/her effectiveness?

_____

_____

_____

29. In your opinion, what more needs to be done to improve his/her area of ministry?

_____

_____

_____

_____

Questions for Evaluation of Parish Ministers

The questions below are suggestions for completing Work Sheets **8-C1** and **8-C2**. Questions related to the person's specific job description and situation may be added.

1. The ability to deal with crises and conflicts.
2. The availability and openness to parishioners.
3. General health and well-being.
4. The sensitivity to special interest or age groups.
5. The interaction with parish groups and individuals.
6. The sensitivity to the needy of the parish and surrounding area.
7. The ability to work with other staff members.
8. The work, as resource person in the parish.
9. The ability to train and supervise volunteers.
10. The resourcing of adult religious education materials.
11. Friendliness to all groups, not playing favorites.
12. The ability to direct administrative and clerical tasks.
13. Sense of humor and ability to accept limitations.
14. The ability to keep in touch with current trends.
15. The interest for the sick and shut-ins of the parish.
16. The coordination of the adult religious education programs.
17. The planning of occasions for adult spiritual growth.
18. The ability to plan attractive adult programs.
19. The selection of music used at the weekend liturgies.
20. The direction/facilitation of congregational singing.
21. The coordination of music for weddings and funerals.
22. The ability to recruit adequate music volunteers.
23. The level of presence and availability at the Masses.
24. The ability to keep in touch with current music trends.
25. The spiritual, prayerful attitude and presence.
26. The overall performance as pastoral associate.
27. How do you rate your knowledge of the pastoral associate?
28. How do you rate your level of involvement in the parish?
29. The interest in the children in the parish.
30. The fostering of religious values among the children.
31. The coordination of the religious education programs.
32. The work as resource person in the parish school.
33. The ability to attract children to the religious education programs.
34. The ability to recruit adequate catechists and teachers.
35. The flexibility to special needs and situations.
36. The management of the religious education budget.
37. The ability to make plans and set goals for the future.
38. The ability to work with other leaders.
39. The level of presence and availability to parents.

8-D

MINISTRY EVALUATION

Fill out the evaluation form from your personal experience of the ministry. Reflections can then be shared with other members of the group.

Area of Ministry: _____

1. What is the overall goal for this area of ministry? What is this ministry trying to accomplish in the long run?

   _____
   _____
   _____
   _____

2. What is one specific goal that we have been trying to accomplish in this area of ministry over the past year?

   _____
   _____
   _____
   _____

3. How close have we come in achieving either our short-range or long-range goals? What progress have we made in the past year?

   _____
   _____
   _____
   _____

4. How has this area of ministry responded to the needs, desires and expectations of those being served?

   _____
   _____
   _____
   _____

5. In your opinion, what's still missing? What still needs to happen so that this area of ministry is meeting its goals and responding to people's needs and expectations?

   _____
   _____
   _____
   _____

6. What, if anything, is getting in the way of progress in this area of ministry, such as, lack of organization, poor meetings, timing, environment, leadership, response, planning, etc?

   _____
   _____
   _____
   _____

Any other comments you may like to make about this area of ministry can be noted on the other side and used for further discussion when the entire group meets to compare notes.

8-E

EVALUATION FORM

There are many different elements that help a group function productively. Rate your personal experience of each of the elements listed below. Share these in the larger group. Find common areas of concern. What can be done to improve the group experience? How will these things be implemented? By whom? When?

Rating Scale: 5 = Excellent, 4 = Good, 3 = Fair, 2 = Poor, 1 = Don't Know

Environment   Further Comments

_____ Room arrangement, spacing, chairs   _____
_____ Physical aspects; light, sound, etc.   _____
_____ Feeling of warmth, comfortableness   _____
_____ Starting and ending on time   _____
_____ Adequate breaks   _____
_____ Time provided for questions, discussion   _____

Leader

_____ Appropriate style of leadership for group   _____
_____ Clear directions and presentation   _____
_____ Use of group dynamics: small groups, etc.   _____
_____ Organization: agenda setting, etc.   _____
_____ Handling tensions and controversies   _____
_____ Ability to adapt to changing situations   _____

Group

_____ Decision-making appropriate to group   _____
_____ Attentiveness to one another and task   _____
_____ Cooperation: no one person dominating   _____
_____ Feeling of accomplishment and worth   _____
_____ Resolution of tension and conflict   _____
_____ Willingness to assume responsibility   _____

Spirit

_____ Enthusiasm and energy level   _____
_____ Sense of purpose and direction   _____
_____ Attention to spiritual dimension   _____
_____ Time for reflection and assimilation   _____
_____ Sense of purpose and common goals   _____
_____ Chance for spirit to continue afterwards   _____

****

_____ Overall Rating (General Impressions)   _____

8-F1

REPORT AND EVALUATION OF A VOLUNTEER MINISTRY

NAME _____ DATE _____

NAME OF MINISTRY POSITION _____

TERM OF THE POSITION: FROM _____   TO _____

1. This ministry position has been satisfying for me because . . .

2. The major frustrations in this ministry position have been . . .

3. I used the following skills in this ministry position . . .

4. The training I received for this position included . . .

5. I felt supported in this position in the following ways . . .

6. I received the following resources which assisted me in this position . . .

7. I would have been able to do this ministry better if . . .

8. The highlights of this ministry for me have been . . .

9. The major accomplishments which have been achieved through this ministry include. . .

10. A person following me in this ministry position needs to know . . .

8-F2

Please rate each of the following as it enabled you to do this ministry effectively and faithfully by placing an "X" where you feel it is most appropriate.

	Outstanding	Average	Inadequate
11. The way in which the position was interpreted and explained to me before I began.			
12. The training I received for doing the ministry.			
13. The support I received from the parish.			
14. The challenge and responsibility I felt in doing this ministry.			
15. The sense of importance the parish places on this ministry.			

The following are about your future volunteer ministries. Please indicate your interests by placing an "X" in the appropriate column.

16. Interest level in a new volunteer ministry:	Very Interested	Interested	Little Interest	No Interest
a. In my parish	___	___	___	___
b. In my community	___	___	___	___
c. In my deanery/diocese	___	___	___	___
d. In an ecumenical setting	___	___	___	___

17. Specific volunteer ministry opportunities I would like to explore:
_____
_____
_____

18. Factors in my situation that would influence my next volunteer ministry position:
Schedule: _____
Transportation: _____
Child care: _____
Other: _____
_____
_____

Copyright © 1983 by Bannon Marketing Associates. <u>Volunteers and Ministry: A Manual for Developing Parish Volunteers</u>. William Bannon and Suzanne Donovan, S.C.. Ramsey, NJ: Paulist Press. Pg. 87-89.

8-G

Evaluation of: _____

Date held: _____ Time: _____ Number of participants: _____

Coordinator(s): _____ Phone: _____
_____ _____

Other contacts: _____ Phone: _____
_____ _____

Publicity used: _____
_____

Physical resources needed: _____
_____
_____

Costs: _____
_____

What worked well: _____
_____
_____

What did not work well: _____
_____
_____

Things to remember for next time: _____
_____
_____
_____